California
Government
and Politics
Today

California Government and Politics Today

ELEVENTH EDITION
Election Update

Mona Field
Glendale Community College

New York   San Francisco   Boston
London   Toronto   Sydney   Tokyo   Singapore   Madrid
Mexico City   Munich   Paris   Cape Town   Hong Kong   Montreal

Editor-in-Chief: Eric Stano
Senior Marketing Manager: Elizabeth Fogarty
Project Coordination, Text Design, and Electronic Page Makeup: Integra
    Software Services Inc.
Senior Cover Design Manager: Nancy Danahy
Cover Designer: Nancy Sacks
Cover Illustration/Photo: © Getty Images, Inc.
Manufacturing Manager: Mary Fischer
Printer and Binder: R.R. Donnelley and Sons
Cover Printer: Phoenix Color Corporation

Library of Congress Cataloging-in-Publication Data

Field, Mona.
    California government and politics today / Mona Field.—11th ed.
        p.   cm.
    Includes bibliographical references and index.
    ISBN 0-321-43654-7
    1. California—Politics and government—1951–   I. Title.

JK8716.F54 2006
320.9794—dc22

                                            2006014764

Please visit us at www.ablongman.com

ISBN 0-205-52115-0

1 2 3 4 5 6 7 8 9 10—DOC—09 08 07 06

Dedication

*For my fathers, Martin Field
and Bob Lees, who lived
their dreams in Hollywood
and helped make California
a better place.*
MONA FIELD

Contents

Contents

Preface

Welcome to the Eleventh Edition of *California Government and Politics Today.* The textbook's mission remains the same: to explain California's ever-changing political situation in the context of social and economic trends. The focus is still on ethnic and cultural diversity, the global economy's impact on California (and vice versa), and the emphasis on political involvement as an essential component of achieving the California dream. While the state is still an economic powerhouse, the current economic climate is uncertain for many individuals, and "pocketbook" or "bread-and-butter" issues drive political trends and moods. This generalized economic anxiety surely contributed to the upheaval of the state's first gubernatorial recall election in 2003 and subsequent events.

Given the rapidly evolving situation in electoral politics, and the continuing roller coaster in state funding for education and other basic needs, it is nearly impossible to produce a fully up-to-date textbook on California government and politics today. However, this book is designed to give a background that enables students to understand fast-changing events. This edition presents some important changes in actual laws, increasing concerns with outsourcing of employment opportunities, the widespread revulsion against negative political campaigns, and the related expansion of "unaffiliated" (decline to state) votes—all of these issues are explored in the context of California's astonishing political landscape.

The book continues to feature numerous charts and maps, a glossary (defining terms that appear in *italics* in the text), a list of useful websites, a section entitled How to Get in Touch with Your Elected Officials, a bibliography for further reading, and a list of political organizations that students may wish to learn more about. In addition, each chapter closes with Questions to Consider, which are a great starting point for class discussions. Students who want to reinforce their learning may go to www.ablongman.com and do interactive self-paced quizzing on each chapter's material. In addition, students can download the detailed Study Guide available through the website; this guide enables students to answer questions as they read.

For the benefit of instructors, a complete test bank is available from your Longman sales representative, in both paper and online versions.

This edition has benefited from the input of colleagues from around the state, including Edgar Kaskla, California State University—Long Beach; Steven Alan Holmes, Bakersfield College; Herbert Gooch, California Lutheran University; and Jodi Balma, Fullerton College. I thank them all for their thoughtful suggestions, which I know have improved the text. I remain personally responsible for the final product, including its strengths and weaknesses. Input and suggestions from colleagues are most welcome, so feel free to contact me directly as you utilize the text and have ideas for improvements.

As always, the goal remains to enlighten our students and support their interest in having their share of the California Dream come true.

MONA FIELD

mfield@glendale.edu

CHAPTER ONE

California Politics in Perspective

"California, after all, is special, a nonstop preview of the future, the cutting edge of the trend that will overtake the country—for good or for ill."

—Susan F. Rasky, University of California, Berkeley, School of Journalism

In yet another example of how California might be the cutting edge of the nation, Governor Schwarzenegger's triumphant re-election in 2006 indicated a wave of public support for bipartisan, moderate leadership. With an eye to projected population growth in years ahead, voters approved billions of dollars of state borrowing for roads, water systems, educational facilities, and affordable housing. Despite the important issues on the ballot, fewer than half of the registered voters showed up to vote.

Californians obviously care about the "quality of life," and those who vote seem willing to create debts for themselves and all future taxpayers in order to rebuild and build the necessary *infrastrucure* for the state. The state's current economy, based on job growth in technology, construction, education, and small business, is never secure, and when the economy takes a downturn, the state and its people once again will worry about how to provide public services.

With its inevitable economic ups and downs, California remains a world economic power: if California were a separate nation it would rank in the top ten nations in gross domestic production. California still leads the nation in population, with hints that by the year 2020 the state will be home to more than 45 million Americans, of whom more than half will be "minorities." (See Table 1.1) But not all Californians are enjoying the

TABLE 1.1

California's Population: Growth Since Statehood

Year	Population
1850	92,597
1860	379,994
1870	560,247
1880	864,694
1890	1,213,398
1900	1,485,053
1910	2,377,549
1920	3,426,861
1930	5,677,251
1940	6,907,387
1950	10,586,223
1960	15,717,204
1970	19,971,069
1980	23,667,902
1990	31,400,000
2003	35,591,000
Projected 2020	45,821,900

Source: U.S. Census Bureau, State Department of Finance.

state's wealth equally. California ranks fifth in the nation in growing income inequality, and the average working family has actually lost income over the past 20 years.[1]

California's status as a *two-tier society,* in which those without adequate education remain caught in low-wage, no-benefits jobs, remains one of the state's biggest challenges. Improving education is a major theme of politicians, but the issue of how to pay for educational excellence remains controversial.

NATIONAL IMPACT: SETTING TRENDS FOR THE COUNTRY

At least in theory, based on the numbers, California remains among the most powerful states in the nation. Being first in population gives California the most members in Congress. The state has 53 of the 435 members of the House of Representatives and 55 *electoral votes,* more than a fifth of the 270 necessary to elect a president. However, having the big numbers is not always the path to national power: the majority of Californians have voted for the losing candidate in the past several presidential elections, so the 55 electoral votes have not made any difference in the national outcome.

Similarly, it would make sense that a state with the nation's largest congressional delegation and the largest bloc of electoral votes should receive the largest share of federal grants, funds, and contracts. Unfortunately for Californians, they are now sending more dollars to Washington, D.C., than they receive back in funds for state and local services. In 2002, California had over 12 percent of the nation's population, contributed over 14 percent of total federal taxes, and received back 11 percent of federal dollars sent to states and localities.[2]

THE STATE AND ITS PEOPLE: POWER BLOCS IN CONFLICT

Like most Americans, Californians are impacted most directly by their state and local political systems. The state determines the grounds for divorce, traffic regulations, public college tuition fees, penalties for drug possession, and qualifications one needs to become a barber, psychologist, or lawyer. It establishes the amount of unemployment compensation, the location of highways, the subjects to be taught in school, and the rates to be charged by telephone, gas, and electric companies. Along with the local governments under its control, it regulates building construction, provides police and fire protection, and spends about 15 percent of the total value of goods and services produced by California residents.

The policy decisions made in these and other areas are influenced by the distribution of political power among various groups with competing needs and aspirations. Some of the power blocs reflect the same conflicts of interest that the nation experiences: labor vs. business; landlords vs.tenants; environmentalists vs. oil companies. But, as in so many things, these battles are fought on a grander scale in California. With its incredibly complex array of local governments, including over 3400 *special districts* to provide everything from street lights to flood control, California's political system almost defies understanding. No wonder that voters have shown their overall mistrust of elected officials and turned to *ballot initiatives* to make new laws and even to amend the state constitution.

These ballot initiatives, or *propositions*, deal with everything from juvenile crime to educational policy, from Indian gaming rights to the ever-present insurance industry issues. While political experts despise the use of initiatives to set public policy, ballot measures are big business. Virtually all propositions are placed on the ballot by *special-interest groups,* either organizations or wealthy individuals. Profitable petition-gathering companies charge several dollars per signature to get issues on the ballot. The outcome of these initiative battles usually depends on such factors as money, media, and the public mood.

THE STATE AND THE FEDERAL SYSTEM: A COMPLEX RELATIONSHIP

Like the other states, California is part of the American federal system. *Federalism* distributes power to both the national and state governments, thereby creating a system of dual citizenship and authority. It is a complex arrangement designed to assure the unity of the country while at the same time permitting the states to reflect the diversity of their people and economies. Although national and state authority overlap in such areas as taxation and highway construction (examples of so-called concurrent powers), each level of government also has its own policy domain. The U.S. Constitution gives the national government its powers, including such areas as immigration law, interstate commerce, foreign policy, national defense, and international relations. The states are permitted to do anything that is not prohibited or that the Constitution does not assign to the national government. Serious conflicts occur when states challenge federal laws, such as California's medical marijuana law, which the current federal government administration insists is unconstitutional despite the law's passage through a voter-approved initiative (Proposition 215, 1996).

Within each state, the distribution of powers is *unitary.* This means that the cities, counties, and other units of local government get their authority from the state. States and their local bodies generally focus their powers on such services as education, public safety, and health and welfare.

Just as California has a mighty impact on the country as a whole, the national government exerts influence on the state. Federal funds often come with strings attached. For example, federal highway funds require specific safety laws, including seatbelt regulations, and even mandate the age at which individuals may purchase alcohol. Meanwhile, the federal government has the power to take over a state system it considers to be failing; in 2006, a U.S. District judge appointed a federal "receiver" to take over the state's prison health-care system.[3]

In some ways, federal policy fuels the state's economy. For nearly 50 years, between World War II and the end of the Cold War, California's private defense industry relied heavily on federal contracts to create a thriving military-based economy. Major corporations, such as Lockheed, Hughes, and Rockwell, enjoyed high profits and provided well-paying, secure jobs to engineers, managers, secretaries, and assembly-line workers. When the Cold War ended in 1989, this entire military contract system was suddenly downsized and many military bases closed, leaving a huge hole in the California economy. In recent years, many of the former federal contractors have reinvented themselves into high-tech businesses,[4] while foreign interventions of the Bush administration have created some new military spending in California. However, the dollar value of current federal defense contracts is small compared to Cold War spending. California continues to seek other sources of economic growth, involving both public and private investment in computer software development, entertainment, tourism, agriculture, and biotechnology, including stem cell research (encouraged by a voter-approved bond measure in 2004).

While relations between the federal government and each state are complex and significant, the relations between states are also important. The U.S. Constitution requires every state to honor the laws of every other state, so that marriages and other contracts made in one state are respected in all states and criminals trying to escape justice cannot find safe haven by leaving the state in which they have been convicted.

Federalism is perhaps America's greatest political invention. It permits states to enact their diverse policy preferences into law on such matters as gambling, prostitution, trash disposal, and wilderness protection, and thus encourages experiments that may spread to other states. California has become known as a place of experimentation, and these new political ideas often spread across the nation. *Conservative* themes such as tax revolts, anti-immigration sentiments, and the backlash against affirmative action all began as successful ballot propositions in California, while *liberal* ideas such as legalization of marijuana for medical purposes and government-provided health care for all also have become ballot battles.

Because federalism allows states great autonomy, and because California has developed a complex web of local governments, the average California voter must make numerous decisions at an election booth. Each Californian, whether or not a U.S. citizen, lives in a number of election jurisdictions, including a congressional district, a state Senate district, an Assembly district, and a county supervisorial district, plus (in most cases) a city, a school district, and a community college district. (See Figure 1.1 for the officials elected by California voters.) This array of political jurisdictions provides many opportunities to exercise democracy. It also creates confusion, overlaps, and many occasions on which voters feel unable to evaluate fully the qualifications of candidates or the merits of ballot propositions.

Other problems linked to federalism include outdated state boundaries that have created some "superstates," with land masses and populations that may be ungovernable, and differences in resources between states. California's large territory could theoretically include two or three states. Meanwhile, variations in states' resources perpetuate inequality in schools, public hospitals, and other government facilities at

Partisan Offices			
National Level	**Elected by**	**Term**	**Election Year**
President	Entire state	4 years	Years divisible by four
U.S. Senators	Entire state	6 years	Every six years counting from 1992
			Every six years counting from 1994
Members of Congress	Districts	2 years	Even-numbered years
State Level			
Governor[1]			
Lt. Governor[1]			
Secretary of State[1]	Entire state	4 years	Even-numbered years when there is no presidential election
Controller[1]			
Treasurer[1]			
Attorney General[1]			
Insurance Commissioner			
Members of Board of Equalization[1]	Districts	4 years	Same as governor
State Senators[1]	Districts	4 years	Same as governor for even-numbered districts
			Same as president for odd-numbered districts
Assembly members[2]	Districts	2 years	Even-numbered years
Nonpartisan Offices			
State Level			
Superintendent of Public Instruction	Entire state	4 years	Same as governor
Supreme Court justices	Entire state	12 years	Same as governor
Court of Appeal justices	Entire state	12 years	Same as governor
Superior Court judges	Counties	6 years	Even-numbered years

[1]Limited to two terms by Proposition 140
[2]Limited to three terms by Proposition 140

FIGURE 1.1 **Federal and State Officials Elected by California Voters**

Source: League of Women Voters.

a time when the nation as a whole is concerned about how to provide these services. The federal system also promotes rivalry between states as they compete to attract new businesses (and jobs) or keep existing ones. Among the tactics used in this struggle are tax breaks, reduced worker compensation, and relaxed environmental protection standards. What remains of California's military-industrial complex, such as Boeing and Lockheed's "Aerospace Valley," must compete for federal contracts against sophisticated efforts from Texas and Missouri.[5] On the larger international scale, the North American Free Trade Agreement (NAFTA) has enhanced the appeal of relocating across the border to Mexico, because goods produced by low-wage labor in Mexican *maquiladoras* can enter the United States with no import tariffs. In today's global economy, California faces tremendous challenges in providing decent jobs, education, health services, and, in general, the high quality of life that the state has always promoted as its chief claim to fame.

QUESTIONS TO CONSIDER

Using Your Text and Your Own Experiences

1. What are some of the pros and cons of life in California? Do these depend in part on whether you live in a rural or an urban area?

2. What are some of the challenges facing our state? What can elected officials do to resolve these challenges? How do you fit into the challenges facing our state?

3. Take a class survey. How many students were born in California? How many are immigrants, either from another state or another nation? Team up so that an "immigrant" is paired with a "native" Californian. Teams or pairs can discuss the different experiences of those born here versus those who immigrated.

ENDNOTES

1. "Legislative Conference Focuses on Wage Gap," *California Labor News*, California Labor Federation, April 2000, p. 1.
2. *Just the Facts: California's Tax Burden*, Public Policy Institute of California, June 2003.
3. Jennifer Warren, "Prison Health Chief Set," *Los Angeles Times*, 12 February 2006, p. B1.
4. Ashley Dunn, "Area's High-Tech Firms Outgrow Military Origins," *Los Angeles Times*, 11 March 2000, p. A1.
5. Andrew Blankstein, "California Joins Fray to Keep Aerospace Alive and Here," *Los Angeles Times*, 28 March 2000, p. A1.

CHAPTER TWO

The Californians: Land, People, and Political Culture

"There will always be a California dream . . . but it won't come with mere wishing. . . . we must all become 'dreamers of the day,' exploring the future with eyes and hearts wide open."

—A. G. Block, journalist

The political process in California, as in other states, is conditioned by many geographic, demographic, and cultural influences. Whereas geography changes only slowly, population shifts and cultural influences can rather suddenly add new and unpredictable threads to the complex web that forms the state's identity and future prospects.

GEOGRAPHIC INFLUENCES: WHERE ARE WE?

With an area of 156,000 square miles, California is larger than Italy, Japan, or England and is the third largest state in the United States, following Alaska and Texas. It is shaped like a gigantic stocking, with a length more than twice its width. If California were superimposed on the East Coast, it would cover six states, from Florida to New York.[1] Despite all the land available, the state's primary urban development has been coastal, with the Bay area and the Los Angeles Basin as the first areas of growth. More recently, the cost of housing has begin creating a "Third California," a region that includes the Inland Empire (San Bernardino/Riverside counties) and the San Joaquin Valley. Relatively affordable homes have created an "eastward surge" of population.[2]

While California's size has contributed to its political dynamics, its location is equally important. As the leading state on what is called the Pacific Rim (those states bordering the Pacific Ocean and facing the Far East), California is the nation's number one exporter. California is also one of only 15 states that border a foreign nation. In part as a result of its proximity to Mexico, Californians of Mexican descent have become the largest ethnic group in the state, one that includes both first-generation Mexican immigrants and "Chicanos," whose parents or ancestors originally came from that country. Nearly half of California's immigrants in recent years have come from Mexico.[3]

Two other geographic influences command attention: rich natural resources and spectacularly beautiful terrain. Between the majestic Sierra Nevada range along the eastern border and the Coastal Mountains on the west lies the Central Valley—one of the richest agricultural regions in the world. Utilizing water supplies brought from the northern section of the state via the California Aqueduct, California leads the nation in farm output, although agriculture's political influence has diminished as agricultural lands have been developed into housing tracts and shopping centers.[4] Water sources and distribution are a perennial battleground, pitting north versus south and rural versus urban areas. Over 40 percent of the state is forested, and this magnificent resource creates tension between the timber industry and environmentalists. California has plentiful oil, some of which lies off the 1000-mile-long coast in locations that have been deemed worthy of permanent protection from offshore drilling.

Although agriculture, timber, and oil remain economically important as well as environmentally controversial, another natural resource has become the subject of continual political debate over how much to exploit it: California's landscape. Ranging across arid deserts, a thousand-mile shoreline, and remote mountain wilderness, the terrain itself is a continuing battlefield between conservationists and commercial recreation developers. Much of California is owned by the public; the state boasts 43 national parks, forests, recreation areas, and monuments, plus its own vast acreage of public forests, parks, and beaches. Despite the huge expanses of undeveloped land, Californians are a largely urban people, with over 80 percent living in cities.[5]

DEMOGRAPHIC INFLUENCES: WHO ARE WE?

With rare, short-term exceptions, modern California has a consistent pattern of rapid population growth. Although some people leave the state to find less expensive places to live, the total number of Californians continues to increase as a result of birth rates (49% of population growth), domestic immigration (11%), and international immigration (40% of total growth).[6] Meanwhile, continuing medical advances keep Californians alive into their 90s, and the senior population is projected to grow to nearly one-third of the total.[7] Long-term predictions suggest that the state will have nearly 50 million people by the year 2030, creating enormous challenges regarding housing, education, health care, transportation, water supplies, and environmental quality. Demographers predict that California will remain the most populous state, with over 12 percent of the nation's people.[8]

California also continues to be the most diverse state, with residents from virtually every nation and ethnic group on the planet. There is no "majority" group, and California has more people who identify themselves as "multiracial" than any other state.[9] (Figure 2.1 breaks down the workforce by ethnic group.) About 25 percent of Californians were born in other nations, with the top three "sending nations" being Mexico, the Philippines, and Vietnam.[10] Despite various federal efforts to reduce illegal border crossings, California still is home to millions of undocumented immigrants, many of whom eventually become legal residents.[11] All population data are questionable, however, because the U.S. Census Bureau acknowledges its inability to accurately count Californians.[12]

Ongoing international immigration adds to the state's socioeconomic gaps, since even two-parent working immigrant families are often living at poverty level, giving California the nation's highest poverty rates.[13] Immigrant communities (and even many individual families) are a

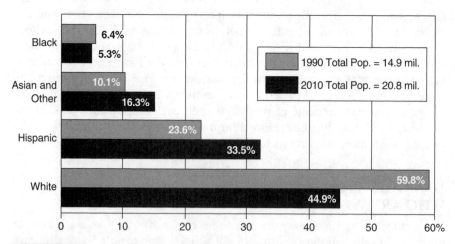

FIGURE 2.1 California Labor Force by Ethnic Group, 1990–2010: Percentage of Labor Force Population

Source: Center for Continuing Study of the California Economy.

complex combination of undocumented immigrants, legal residents, political refugees, and foreign-born naturalized U.S. citizens. Many immigrants spend years in paperwork as they wait for the federal Bureau of Citizenship and Immigration Services (formerly known as the Immigration and Naturalization Service) to process their applications and move them from refugee status to legal resident, or from resident to citizen status. Both legal and illegal immigrants who are not citizens make up nearly 20 percent of Californians, none of whom can vote, yet all of whom are affected by electoral decisions.[14] During the transition years, *assimilation* takes place to varying degrees, as individuals decide whether to learn English, how much education to seek, and how much to "Americanize" their customs.

Whether they are citizens or residents, concentrations of immigrant ethnic groups have already altered the social and political landscape in many California communities. Out of choice or necessity, ethnic enclaves develop wherever a group puts down roots, their presence reflected in the language of storefront signs, distinctive architecture, and types of food available. Daly City is called "Little Manila," and Fresno is home to 30,000 Hmong, members of a Laotian hill tribe. Sacramento has a large Slavic community; Stockton has 35,000 refugees from several areas of Indochina; Glendale has a substantial concentration of Armenians; Westminster, in Orange County, has a section known as "Little Saigon;" and Monterey Park, the first city in the continental United States with an Asian majority,[15] is 56 percent Chinese. One-fourth of the children in California's public schools are considered "English learners," with some large school districts serving as many as 80 language groups.[16]

During *recessions*, when job losses and related fears of the future create anxiety, negativity against immigrants sometimes rises, and both immigrants and American-born ethnic minorities may become victims of harassment or prejudice. Because people often judge others based on appearance, American-born Latinos and Asians may be subject to prejudices and discrimination based on either ethnic stereotypes or anti-immigrant attitudes. Meanwhile, African-Americans, the third largest ethnic minority group, continue to see their numbers decline in proportion to the fast-growing Latino and Asian communities, with resulting concerns about how blacks can compete successfully for educational, economic, and political opportunities while other ethnic groups begin to dominate numerically.

Population diversity, of course, embraces far more than ethnicity. Collectively, Californians seem to embody virtually the whole range of religious beliefs, including nearly 20 percent who profess no religion at all. California, being 45 percent Protestant, 25 percent Roman Catholic, 5 percent Jewish, and 7 percent "other," has no "majority religion." About one-third of Californians claim to be "born-again

Christians," which may partially account for the strength of the Christian Coalition, a political movement based on the belief that fundamentalist Christian theology should guide American politics.[17]

Another of California's diverse groupings is the gay community, often a target of fundamentalist Christians. Although most Californians have a "live and let live" attitude toward people's sexual orientation, political battles still occur regarding gay marriage, the rights of gay or lesbian couples to adopt children, and the general recognition of gay, lesbian, bisexual, and transgendered (*GLBT*) individuals. Gay bashing, a form of violent hostility (and a hate crime), in which an individual is attacked for his or her perceived sexual orientation, brings tragic consequences and outrage. Though still a distinct minority, the five-member GLBT caucus of the state legislature includes legislators who are openly homosexual and who unite to represent this portion of the population.

CALIFORNIA'S POLITICAL CULTURE: HOW WE THINK

Each state has a distinctive political style that is shaped not only by its geography and population characteristics but also by the values and attitudes shared by most of its people. These elements constitute what is sometimes called the political culture. In many ways, California is similar to the rest of the country and is conditioned by the same influences. Californians embrace the principles of patriotism, capitalism, and democracy as fervently as other Americans do. But there are differences as well, stemming from both unique historical development and the steady emergence of distinctive problems demanding political attention. California's frontier heritage, for example, includes a legacy of materialistic individualism that may exceed that of most other states.

Perhaps this focus on the freedom to cash in and acquire the status symbols of the California life (a pool, a Porsche, and a private school for the kids) has made California more of a *two-tier* state than some others. In fact, California is multitiered, with huge gaps between those at the top and those at the bottom of the income levels (See Figure 2.2.). The major cause of vast inequalities in household incomes is the increasing gap between private corporate salaries and the low-wage working poor. The incomes of the wealthiest 5 percent of families increased by 50 percent between the late 1970s and late 1990s, while the poorest fifth of the state's families lost 5 percent of their income during the same period.[18] Middle-income families are not protected from economic woes; their sense of security is jeopardized by high housing costs and the continuing loss of midlevel income opportunities.[19]

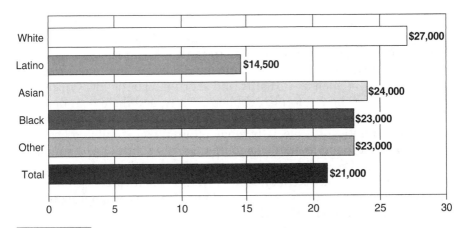

FIGURE 2.2 Median Wage Income in California

Sources: California Research Bureau, San Francisco Chronicle Survey; *California Journal,* March 2000, p. 32.

Large socioeconomic gaps are aggravated for all Californians by the extremely high cost of housing,[20] inadequate health care for the one-fifth of Californians who are uninsured, and the increasing competition for higher-education opportunities. Economic recession and state budget cuts have raised costs for public higher education substantially, while public health-care options are seriously underfunded by cash-strapped counties. These facts are hard to reconcile with one of the world's strongest economies, which theoretically should be able to provide better for its people.

With all the economic and social difficulties they face, it's no surprise that Californians may use their votes to show serious frustration with their political leaders, most recently through the gubernatorial *recall* election and the unpopular special election called by Governor Schwarzenegger (November 2005) in which all eight ballot measures were defeated. California's electorate continues to be mostly white, older, and more affluent, even though the population of the state is diverse, young, and of moderate or low income. Even with a large push for "vote by mail," in which people vote by mailing in their ballot before election day, and with some counties experimenting with touch-screen voting, potential voters too often ignore their opportunity to determine electoral outcomes.

Although not all eligible citizens bother to vote, the recognition of government's power motivates many Californians to form political associations to represent their views. Because of the ethnic, socioeconomic, and cultural diversity of the state, California is home to a wide variety of political organizations. The ideologies behind the organizations can be simplistically summarized by the traditional labels of American politics: conservative and liberal. The *conservative* side of California politics is torn between those who support maximum freedom for both business and individuals and those who like free enterprise but prefer government to regulate personal behavior such as sexuality and abortion. These uneasy partners form the basis of the California Republican Party, and their areas of agreement often end with tax cuts and calls to *privatize* government services. Moderate Republicans, especially women, often feel conflicted between their views on economic matters and their party's continuing domination by "cultural conservatives," who promote an antichoice, antigay, and antifeminist agenda. Republican Governor Schwarzenegger, who campaigned as pro-business, antitax, and pro-choice, is attempting to pull the two groups together within the GOP.

On the other side of the political spectrum, the *liberal* movement in California has gained some prominent champions, such as Los Angeles Mayor Antonio Villaraigosa, who actively promotes the value of government serving to improve people's lives. Some of the liberal idealism rooted in California's history has lived on in efforts to get "living wages" for city employees, government-sponsored health care for all, and public investment in alternative fuels. But political labels are only one aspect of California's complex polity: many Californians are uninterested in traditional political labels and, in the noble American pragmatic tradition, just want to solve problems. At the moment, the Golden State has plenty of problems to face and resolve.

QUESTIONS TO CONSIDER

Using Your Text and Your Own Experiences

1. What is the relationship between California's geography (size, location, topography, etc.) and its economic and political situation?

2. What are some of the pros and cons of the state's ethnic diversity?

3. Discuss the issue of social and economic inequality. What problems are caused by the vast gaps between rich and poor? Are there any advantages to having a two-tier society?

ENDNOTES

1. *Los Angeles Times*, 17 December 1987, Part 1, p. 3.
2. Joel Kotkin and William Frey, "The Third California," *Los Angeles Times*, 29 January 2006, p. M1.
3. Laura E. Hill and Joseph M. Hayes, "California's Newest Immigrants," *California Counts*, Public Policy Institute of California, Vol. 5, No. 2, November 2003, p. 1.

4. "Competition for Land," *American Farmland,* American Farmland Trust, Fall 1996, p. 5.
5. "81% of Californians Live in Cities, State Agency Says," *Los Angeles Times,* 5 May 1999, p. A38.
6. California Department of Finance, *Population Growth by Types of Sources, 2000–2004,* cited in Southern California Association of Governments, The State of the Region 2005, December 2005.
7. Sonya M. Tafoya and Hans P. Johnson, "Graying in the Golden State," *California Counts,* Public Policy Institute of California, Vol. 2, No. 2, November 2000, p. 1
8. Hans P. Johnson, "How Many Californians? A Review of Population Projections for the State," *California Counts,* Public Policy Institute of California, Vol. 1, No. 1, October 1999, p. 1.
9. Solomon Moore, "State Leads Nation in Mixed-Race Individuals," *Los Angeles Times,* 29 November 2001, p. B8.
10. Hill and Hayes, "California's Newest Immigrants," p. 3.
11. Ricardo Alonso-Zaldivar, "Number of Illegal Migrants Growing," *Los Angeles Times,* 1 February 2003, p. A15.
12. Robin Fields, "State Census Sampling Shows Huge Undercount," *Los Angeles Times,* 7 December 2002, p. B10.
13. Mary C. Daly, Deborah Reed, and Heather N. Royer, "Population Mobility and Income Inequality in California," *California Counts,* Public Policy Institute of California, Vol. 2, No. 4, May 2001. p. 1
14. Joaquin Avila, *Latino Policy and Issues Brief,* UCLA Chicano Studies Research Center, No. 9, December 2003, p. 1.
15. Seth Mydans, "Asian Investors Create a Pocket of Prosperity," *New York Times,* 17 October 1994, p. A8.
16. Sonya M. Tafoya, "The Linguistic Landscape of California Schools," *California Counts,* Public Policy Institute of California, Vol. 3, No. 4, February 2002, p. 1
17. Mark Nollinger, "The New Crusaders: The Christian Right Storms California's Political Bastions," *California Journal,* January 1993, p. 6.
18. "Boom, Bust and Beyond: The State of Working California," California Budget Project, 2003.
19. Stuart Silverstein and Lee Romney, "Middle-Class Families Put in Economic Bind," *Los Angeles Times,* 6 August 2001, p. B1.
20. Steven F. Hayward, "Preserving the American Dream: The Facts about Suburban Communities and Housing Choice," California Building Industry Association/Building Industry Institute, September 1996.

■ ■ ■ ■ ■

CHAPTER THREE

California's Historical Development

"Throughout its American history, California has been
a population accumulation zone without parallel."
—James D. Houston, California scholar

California's modern history begins with the native population of about 300,000 people in approximately 100 linguistic/cultural "tribelets," who lived on this land before the Europeans arrived.[1] Despite the unique culture of each of the dozens of Native California tribes, very little information exists regarding the diverse groups that inhabited California during this period. Perhaps that is because these first Californians were nearly exterminated. According to a New York newspaper in 1860, "in [other] States, the Indians have suffered wrongs and cruelties. . . . But history has no parallel to the recent atrocities perpetrated in California. Even the record of Spanish butcheries in Mexico and Peru has nothing so diabolical."[2] The hunter-gatherers of California were soon annihilated to make room for the *conquistadores*, whose desire for gold led them to murder and rape many of the people they found here.[3]

THE SPANISH ERA: 1542–1822

In 1542, only 50 years after Columbus first came to the "New" World, Spain claimed California as a result of a voyage by Juan Rodriguez Cabrillo. More than two centuries passed, however, before the Spanish established their first colony. It was named San Diego and was founded by an expedition headed by Gaspar de Portola, a military commander, and Junipero Serra, a missionary dedicated to converting the Indians to Roman Catholicism. Between 1769 and 1823, the Spanish conquerors built 22 missions from San Diego to Sonoma, each with its own military post. By the time the missions were completed, most of the Native Californians had been destroyed by overwork, disease, and brutality. Meanwhile, farther south, the *mestizo* residents of New Spain (primarily what is now Mexico, Central America, and many of the Spanish-speaking South American colonies) were ready to overthrow the Spanish colonial rulers and declare independence.

MEXICAN DOMINANCE: 1821–1848

In 1821, Mexico won independence from Spain. Soon after, the land now called California (as well as the modern states of Utah, Colorado, New Mexico, and Arizona) officially became part of the new United States of Mexico. Civilian governments were established for the pueblos, or villages, but the distant government in Mexico City still viewed California as a remote and relatively unimportant colony.

American settlers began to arrive in the 1840s, lured by the inviting climate and stories of economic opportunities. Many were filled with the spirit of *manifest destiny*, a belief that Americans had a mission to control the whole continent. When the United States failed in its attempt to buy California, it used a Texas boundary dispute as an excuse to launch war with Mexico in 1846. The United States declared victory within a year, thus winning the right to purchase at bargain rates enormous lands including California, Arizona, New Mexico, and Texas, as well as large parts of Utah, Colorado, and Nevada. California came under American military rule, and in 1848 Mexico renounced its claims by signing the Treaty of Guadalupe Hidalgo, a document that promised the Mexican population of California that their language and property would be respected under the new government—a promise that was quickly broken. Within a short time, the ranchos of the *Californios* (people of Mexican descent) were grabbed by immigrants (mostly Anglos), and much of these lands were later granted to the owners of the railroads.[4]

AMERICANIZATION AND STATEHOOD: 1848–1850

The U.S. military occupation lasted three years while Congress battled over how to manage its vast new territories. The turning point was the discovery of gold in 1848, encouraging "Forty-niners" from all over the world to head to California. By 1849, the population quadrupled, and the settlers adopted the first California constitution. Meanwhile, the U.S. Congress postponed the Civil War through enacting the Compromise of 1850 (which kept a balance of slave and free states) by admitting California as a free state. California became the thirty-first state and the first that did not border an existing state. (Figure 3.1 shows the county boundaries of California today.)

FIGURE 3.1 **Map of California**

Source: Los Angeles County Almanac, 1991.

Today the legacy of the Spanish and Mexican periods can be found in California's population itself, as well as in the missions, architecture, and city names. History does not easily erase itself; California's Spanish/Mexican roots pervade the culture.

CONSOLIDATING POWER: 1850–1902

During its first 50 years of statehood, California grew in both population and diversity. Newcomers from around the world came to seek their fortunes, and some were extraordinarily successful. Others, particularly during economic downturns, began to *scapegoat* less popular groups and call for their expulsion. Chinese immigrants, brought to this country to build the railroads cheaply, were major targets of overt racism and discrimination during the recession of the 1870s. Despite occasional downturns, the overall economy boomed during the 1880s and 1890s, although the *Californios* generally became impoverished and forgotten as white Americans took charge. The economy shifted from mining to agriculture, and the arrival of the transcontinental railroad brought people from across the nation eager to begin new lives and find a share of California's richness.

In 1879, the first state constitution was replaced by the one now in effect. In a preview of political events that seem to recur every time the state's economy sags, the second California constitution was loaded with anti-immigrant provisions (aimed at Asian immigrants), which were later declared invalid as violations of the U.S. Constitution.

THE PROGRESSIVE LEGACY: 1902–1919

The *Progressive movement* in California, like its national counterpart, arose at the beginning of the twentieth century. Its goal was to reduce the power of corrupt political parties and rich corporations that spent large sums to control politicians. In California, the primary target was the Southern Pacific Railroad, a corporation that owned one-fifth of all nonpublic land in the state. Its major stockholders—Charles Crocker, Leland Stanford, Collis P. Huntington, and Mark Hopkins—were the "Big Four" of state politics. According to their critics, they had bought "the best state legislature that money could buy."

Despite the power of the Big Four, the Progressives had remarkable success. Child labor laws and conservation policies were adopted. Political parties were weakened by imposing rigid legal controls on their internal organization and prohibiting candidates for city, county, and judicial offices and education boards from mentioning their party affiliation on the ballot. Today, all of these offices remain *nonpartisan*, with only names and occupations listed on the ballot.

Possibly the most important legacies left by the Progressives were the *direct democracy* powers that permit voters to pass laws or amend the state constitution through the ballot box, as well as to recall elected officials from office through a special election. The Progressive reforms of 1911 also brought suffrage to California women, nine years before they won the right to vote in federal elections.

THE TWENTIETH CENTURY, CALIFORNIA STYLE

In the last century, California experienced many of the same major events as the rest of the nation: the Roaring Twenties, the Great Depression, the World War II economic boom. California's contributions to American history of these periods includes the near election of a socialist governor in 1934 (and the *redbaiting* campaign to defeat him), the *Depression-era migration* of hundreds of thousands of people from the Midwest Dust Bowl to the "Golden State," and the *repatriation* of 600,000 U.S. citizens of Mexican descent who were deported from California as official scapegoats for the economic woes of the era.[5] During World War II, Japanese Californians were deported to detention "camps," and their homes and businesses were confiscated as they became the target of wartime scapegoating. When the economy boomed during the Cold War, new arrivals were once again welcomed to help develop the aerospace/defense industries. Throughout the century, through good and bad times, California's population continued to grow.

The long period of relative prosperity during the 1950s and 1960s did not touch everyone. When cheap labor was needed in the agricultural fields during World War II, for example, Mexican *braceros* entered the country with temporary work permits but were expelled when their labor was no longer needed.[6] People of color experienced discrimination in housing, employment, and education. By the early 1960s, California's educational system was rocked by the street protests of UC Berkeley students protesting their own lack of free speech on campus as well as the unequal treatment of blacks in Bay Area businesses.[7] By the end of the 1960s, California was known as the center of a counterculture of drugs, antiwar sentiment, and sexual experimentation in places like San Francisco's Haight-Ashbury neighborhood.

During the *inflationary* period of the 1970s, Californians, enraged by the rapid increases in prices of everything from gasoline to property taxes, voted their frustration by supporting the deep property tax cuts of Proposition 13 (1978). By the 1980s, former California Governor Ronald Reagan was president of the United States and the economy again boomed, although the promised "trickle-down" of economic improvements to the poor did not occur. Most recently, the economic pendulum has swung rapidly from *recession* (1990–1995) to prosperity (1996–2001) and then back again to recession (2001–2005). These rapid economic shifts have contributed to political upheavals such as the state's historic *gubernatorial* recall election (2003) and to the continuing budget difficulties in our state and local governments.

CALIFORNIA'S CONSTITUTION: A FEW HIGHLIGHTS

Like the national government, the California political system is characterized by a separation of powers, freedom, and democracy. Certain differences, however, deserve attention. Although the separation of powers involves the traditional three branches—legislative, executive, and judicial—each is marked by distinctive state characteristics. For example, the California legislature shares lawmaking authority with the people through the *initiative* process; the governor's power is diminished by the popular election of seven other executive officials; and California judges must be approved by voters. The federal system has none of the *direct democracy* features, nor do federal judges ever appear on the ballot.

Many of the freedoms guaranteed in the state constitution are identical to those protected by the U.S. Constitution. However, the state constitution includes additional rights for its residents. For example, Article I, Section 1, of the California constitution proclaims that "All people are by nature free and independent and have inalienable rights. Among these are enjoying and defending life and liberty, acquiring, possessing, and protecting property, and pursuing and obtaining safety, happiness, and privacy." Similar references to property acquisition, safety, happiness, and privacy do not exist in the U.S. Constitution.

California's constitution is much easier to amend than the federal Constitution, and it has been amended (and thus lengthened) over 500 times since 1879. The process involves two steps. First, amendments may be proposed either by a two-thirds vote in both houses of the legislature or by an *initiative* petition signed by 8 percent of the number of voters who voted in the last election for governor. Second, the proposed amendment must appear as a *proposition* on the ballot and must be approved by a simple majority of voters. As a result of the options created by the Progressives, voters can amend the state constitution without any legislative action.

Because the authors of initiative measures, as well as the voters, rarely distinguish between propositions that create laws and those that amend the constitution, the document has been burdened with many policies that should be *statutes* rather than parts of the permanent state charter. Over the years, the state constitution has become excessively long and detailed, and because so many aspects of state government seem to be inefficient or unresponsive to the public, there are periodic Constitutional Revision Commission reports that attempt to develop major changes to the document. However, these reports are rarely fully implemented. For the foreseeable future, it appears that California's constitution will remain as oversized and complex as its territory and population.

QUESTIONS TO CONSIDER

Using Your Text and Your Own Experiences

1. Who were the first Californians? Why and how were they almost totally destroyed by those who came next?

2. What is the most important contribution of the Progressive movement in California? How would the Progressives feel about contemporary California politics?

3. What are some ways that California's history impacts life today, including culture, politics, ethnic diversity, and immigration?

ENDNOTES

1. Sucheng Chan and Spencer C. Olin, *Major Problems in California History*, (New York: Houghton Mifflin, 1997), p. 30.
2. Cited by Alexander Cockburn, "Beat the Devil," *The Nation*, 24 June 1991, p. 839.
3. Antonia I. Castaneda, "Spanish Violence Against Amerindian Women," in Adela de la Torre and Beatriz Pasquera, eds., *Building with Our Hands: New Directions in Chicano Studies*, (Berkeley: University of California Press, 1993).
4. "Conflicts over Land in a New State, 1850s–1870s," in Chan and Olin, eds., *Major Problems in California History*, pp. 110–135.
5. Gregg Jones, "Reparations Sought for '30s Expulsion Program," *Los Angeles Times*, 16 July 2003, p. B8.
6. Stephanie S. Pincetl, *Transforming California: A Political History of Land Use and Development*, (Baltimore MD: Johns Hopkins University Press, 1999), p. 174.
7. W. J. Rorabaugh, "Berkeley in the 1960s," in Chan and Olin, eds., *Major Problems in California History*, pp. 375–384.

CHAPTER FOUR

Freedom and Equality: California's Delicate Balance

"California is not so much poor as it is unequal."
—Robert Enoch Buck, sociologist

People in California, as everywhere else in a capitalist democracy, must continually reassess choices regarding personal freedom and social equality. *Civil liberties,* such as freedoms of speech, press, and association (which restrict government powers), may conflict with *civil rights,* which often require government protections. For example, freedom of association can conflict with antidiscriminatory civil rights laws. Even though the state's Unruh Civil Rights Act was passed in 1959, some clubs and individuals are still claiming First Amendment freedom as reason to exclude women, unmarried couples, atheists, and homosexuals. Traditionally *underrepresented* ethnic groups and socioeconomically disadvantaged communities continue to battle unequal conditions. Battles over civil rights and civil liberties are fought in the courts through lawsuits, in the legislature through lawmaking, and at the voting booth through *initiatives.* Students sue the state over unequal conditions in public schools; legislators work on issues regarding reparations for American citizens who were expelled from California as scapegoats for various economic and political issues; and voters decide issues such as Proposition 54 (October 2003), a measure to prevent government agencies and schools from collecting data about an individual's race or ethnicity.

FREEDOM AND SOCIAL RESPONSIBILITY: JUGGLING BETWEEN EXTREMES

In numerous areas where individual freedom (or corporate profits) may conflict with public needs, California's policies have moved from supporting maximum personal freedom to placing some limits on that freedom in order to maximize the well-being of the larger society. Antismoking laws, helmet laws for motorcyclists and children on bicycles, and strict regulations for teen drivers all indicate the state's interest in protecting individuals from each other. In the area of personal privacy (often violated by telemarketers and other businesses), the legislature has struggled to create privacy protections as well to protect Californians from cyberstalking and identity fraud.[1] In the arena of environmental quality, the traditional struggle between public well-being and business profitability fluctuates between cooperative approaches and outright political battles. A cooperative effort between environmentalists and major industries led to the San Joaquin Valley Air Pollution Control District's study in 2000 regarding sources of smog in the Central Valley, with an understanding that all sides would benefit from better air quality.[2] In a less collaborative situation, the Los Angeles Regional Water Quality Control Board denied the business community's appeals about high costs and demanded that all new building developments include plans to collect or filter rainwater so that polluted rainwaters would not end up in local beaches.[3]

In another arena of personal rights, California courts have ruled that individual freedom includes the right *not* to hear a prayer at a public school graduation ceremony. In deference to the vast diversity of religious beliefs among Californians, the state Supreme Court determined that such prayers and invocations are an establishment of religion in violation of the separation of church and state. Despite this ruling, many public schools still offer prayers at football games, graduations, and other tax-sponsored events.

EQUALITY: A CONTINUING CHALLENGE

California's large gaps between wealth and poverty inevitably create vast inequality among individuals. Compounding this socioeconomic inequality, Californians have also been forced to confront a long history of inequality based on racial bigotry. Prejudicial attitudes and discriminatory behaviors are older than the state itself. Only 10 percent of the Native Californians survived the Spanish era, and the first governor after statehood called for the extermination of those who remained. When the United States defeated Mexico in 1848, California Mexicans were gradually marginalized, losing much of the political and economic power

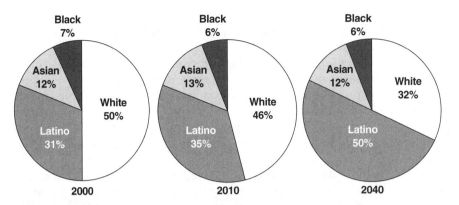

FIGURE 4.1 Projected Ethnic Breakdown of California's Population

Source: California Department of Finance, 1998.

they once wielded. Soon after, in the period of economic stagnation of the 1870s, the Chinese immigrants who helped build the transcontinental railroads during the 1860s became the targets of serious forms of racism, including lynchings and the "Chinese exclusion" provision of the 1879 state constitution (which attempted to prohibit Chinese from holding many kinds of jobs).

In today's multicultural California, the issues of equity are more complex than ever. (See Figure 4.1 for California's major population groups.) Although Proposition 209 ended all forms of *affirmative action* in public education and state systems, California is far from the "color-blind" utopia to which opponents of affirmative action aspire. Wage gaps clearly divide whites and Asians from African-Americans and Latinos, with whites and Asians generally earning more than African-Americans and Latinos, primarily owing to the lower educational attainments of the latter two ethnic groups. (See Figure 4.2.) A vicious cycle in which lack of educational opportunities leads to continuing underemployment can extend from generation to generation.

Perhaps it is the underlying economic gaps that add to racial and ethnic tensions. These prejudices exist not only between whites and various minorities, but among minority groups themselves. In urban school districts, high schools may be homes to competing ethnic gangs whose rivalry erupts in periodic violence between some combination of Latinos, African-Americans, Asians, or Middle Eastern ethnic groups. Inside California's vast prison system, inmates of different ethnic groups were segregated to avoid racial violence until the U.S. Supreme Court declared this racial separation unconstitutional in 2005.

The conflicts among many of California's ethnic groups reflect in part the continuing difficulties created by competition for scarce opportunities. Although the law prohibits discrimination in employment, subtle limitations exist for nonwhite groups. In the rapidly expanding and highly competitive entertainment industry, opportunities for people of color continue to be rare. Despite the handful of well-known blacks and Latinos in the field, membership statistics for both the Writers Guild of America and the Screen Actors Guild indicate the work yet to be done on fully integrating these potentially lucrative fields. In a very different industry, as recently as spring 2000, a federal judge ordered shipping companies and the longshore union to pay nearly $3 million in damages to hundreds of minorities who failed a biased employment test used to determine who could become a dockworker.[4]

Additional scarce opportunities for many Californians occur in the area of housing. Housing affordability in California has dropped substantially as housing costs soar and incomes cannot keep up with prices. The California Association of Realtors reports that only 16% of California households can afford the median-priced home.[5] These costs have forced many low-income households into substandard and overcrowded rental housing, in both urban and rural areas.

Adequate housing also may determine educational opportunities, because public school quality varies in different neighborhoods. Education is the key to a lifetime of increased economic opportunity. The combination of underfunded schools, overcrowding in urban areas, and *white flight* leaves many public school systems with 90 percent nonwhite students, of whom large numbers may need English-language instruction as well as all the core courses. Private schools, public school magnets, and the growing number of charter schools frequently serve higher income or highly motivated families and may contribute to the continuing *class gap*. Test scores, graduation rates, college admission data, and other indicators of educational success are almost always lower at public schools, which are attended predominantly by Latinos and African-Americans (typically from low-income families). Figure 4.2 shows high school completion rates.

Even if California's youth have the qualifications to enter universities, or the motivation to attend a public two-year college (where there are no academic admission requirements), huge fee increases at the two public university systems as well as the community colleges make it harder for low-income Californians to achieve higher education. Financial aid is available, but many eligible Californians do not realize they can get help to achieve their college goals.

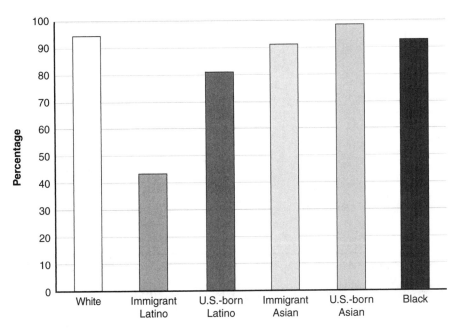

FIGURE 4.2 **California's High School Completion Rates, 1999**
Source: Public Policy Institute of California.

DIVERSITY IN REPRESENTATION: IDENTITY POLITICS IN ACTION

In a continuing American tradition, when ethnic and immigrant communities grow larger, they begin to fight for their share of political and economic power. California's growing ethnic communities have already shifted the demographic pattern: there is no longer any one "majority" group. By the year 2021, it is predicted that whites will make up about one-third of the population and thus will be a "minority" group, while Latinos, Asians, and blacks together will make up 60 percent (40%, 14%, and 6%, respectively).[6] However, this *demographic shift* does not automatically create an equally rapid shift in political power. Gains for underrepresented groups depend on much more than their population count. Factors that influence access to political power include their rates of voter registration and turnout, their financial ability to support candidates, and their interest in the political process. However, at current levels of voter participation and citizenship among foreign-born immigrants, it is expected that by 2040, whites would represent only 35 percent of voting-age adults but would still be 53 percent of the electorate.[7]

In addition to the issues of citizenship and participation in voting, another factor in political success is the use of financial resources to support candidates and influence elections. Because average house-hold

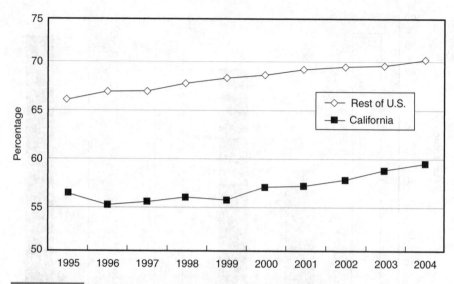

FIGURE 4.3 **Homeownership Rates, 1995–2004**
Source: Public Policy Institute of California.

income is lower for many ethnic communities, they do not have the disposable income to support or recruit their own candidates. Coalitions of ethnic groups, including whites, have emerged as a way to promote qualified candidates from a variety of ethnic groups. In keeping with their rapidly increasing population numbers, the number of Latino and Asian-American elected officials has grown, and in some communities, city council and school board members increasingly include immigrant politicians eager to be involved in their new country as elected leaders.[8]

One interethnic issue facing the growing number of politically active Latinos (and Asians to a lesser degree) is the high numbers of Latinos moving into formerly African-American neighborhoods. Formerly black communities now often are numerically dominated by Latinos, particularly immigrant Latinos. Census data suggest that African-Americans (like whites) will decline numerically in proportion to the much faster growing Latino and Asian groups, African-American leaders are therefore concerned about maintaining adequate electoral representation in places like South Los Angeles and Oakland. Some black politicians have made it a point to learn Spanish, as a way to improve their connections with their Latino constituents.

Providing better political representation to Latinos through language acquisition is relatively simple because most Latinos have Spanish-language origins, although they may represent any one of 18 different nationalities. In contrast, Asian-Americans represent over 30 distinct national and language origins, with the largest populations being Filipino, Chinese, Korean, and Vietnamese. Because the diversity is so enormous, there will never be precise and proportional representation for every ethnic group. Therefore, elected officials, regardless of their own background, must learn to represent everyone and not appeal to narrow ethnic concerns.

In addition to the largest ethnic and racial groups, small but active minority communities are working toward gaining a greater share of political power. Armenian-Californians have seen a governor from their heritage elected, while California's growing Islamic population seeks better access to the political process, especially since negative stereotyping and hate crimes have created real fears among some Muslim communities. Native Californians, who compose over 120 tribal groups, have focused their political attention and substantial campaign contributions on issues relating to economic development on tribal land (with a heavy emphasis on building gambling casinos) and protection of their culture. With the state's social diversity likely to continue, political leadership in the twenty-first century will be a rainbow of cultures, all of which might retain their unique identities while also working to represent all Californians.

SEXUAL POLITICS: SLOW CHANGE FOR THE UNDERREPRESENTED

Women have made slow progress since the Women's Liberation movement of the 1960s raised concerns about women's equality and access to power. Although women account for 51 percent of the population, they are nowhere near holding half of the legislative seats, executive positions, judgeships, or local posts available. After some gains for women in the 1990s, the number of women in the state legislature has dropped, perhaps owing to the enormous time demands of running for office and fund-raising. The state Supreme Court now has three (out of seven) women. Meanwhile, at the nonelected level, thousands of women who are state employees in agencies ranging from the Department of Motor Vehicles to the Employment Development Department earn only about three-fourths as much as men doing the same jobs.[9] In one unfortunate measure of *parity*, the number of women has increased in the state prison system, almost doubling since 1990.[10]

California was the first state to elect two women to the U.S. Senate, Barbara Boxer and Dianne Feinstein, and the home of the first woman Speaker of the House, Nancy Pelosi (D–San Francisco). They are joined in Washington, D.C., by 18 other women in the House of Representatives. Since there are currently no term limits for federal officials, the women in Congress may remain in office for many years.

One often invisible and certainly underrepresented minority group (made up of individuals of all ethnicities) is the gay and lesbian community. At one time, openly gay politicians were rare outside of San Francisco or West Hollywood, both magnets for the homosexual population. Now, as noted earlier, the state legislature has five men and women in its Gay, Lesbian, Bisexual, and Transgender (GLBT) caucus, and numerous local governments have gay and lesbian elected officials. As more gays come *out of the closet* and become politically active, their clout will no doubt increase. However, the gay community has *partisan* differences, with gay Republicans fighting hard for respect in their party and gay Democrats emphasizing the supportiveness of their party's policies.

California's record of electing politicians with diverse backgrounds is certainly better than that of many other states. But perhaps it is inevitable that California will take the lead, since the demographic pattern of increasing diversity is unlikely to change, and trends suggest that the nation will gradually become more like California.

QUESTIONS TO CONSIDER

Using Your Text and Your Own Experiences

1. Discuss some areas where individual freedom (or free enterprise) may conflict with social needs. What is your position on these issues?

2. In what arenas are ethnic "minorities" underrepresented? Why do these patterns persist even though California has no "majority" group?

3. What can be done to balance the needs of diverse ethnic groups with the needs of California as a whole?

ENDNOTES

1. "California Laws 1999," *Los Angeles Times*, 1 January 1999, p. A3.
2. Eric Bailey, "Central Valley Looking for Ways to Fight Air Pollution," *Los Angeles Times*, 6 June 2000, p. A3.
3. Joe Mozingo, "Officials Seek to Ease Fears on Plan to Curb Storm Runoff," *Los Angeles Times*, 9 June 2000, p. B3.
4. Dan Weikel, "$2.75 Million Ordered Paid to Minorities in Dockworker Case," *Los Angeles Times*, 10 June 2000, p. B1.
5. Hans P. Johnson and Amanda Bailey, *California Counts*, Public Policy Institute of California, Vol. 7, No. 1, August 2005, p. 3.
6. Armando Acuna, "Changes in State's Ethnic Balance Are Accelerating," *Los Angeles Times*, 20 October 1999, p. A3.

7. Jack Citrin and Benjamin Highton, "When the Sleeping Giant Is Awake," *California Journal*, December 2002, p. 44.
8. Teresa Watanabe, "Chinese Take to U.S. Politics," *Los Angeles Times*, 8 April 2003, p. B1.
9. "State's Female Workers Paid Less Than Men, Study Finds," *Los Angeles Times*, 25 April 1996, p. A21.
10. Jennifer Warren, "Plan Puts Female Inmates in Centers by Their Families," *Los Angeles Times*, 11 February 2006, p. A1.

CHAPTER FIVE

Media Influences and Interest Groups

"California is the Wild, Wild West for influence-peddling greased by campaign cash, self-dealing and insider connections."

> —Jamie Court, President, Foundation for Taxpayer and Consumer Rights

I n a democratic system, the attitudes of the public should be a primary basis for political decision making. These political attitudes are demonstrated in election results and develop from opinions formed by the influence of families, friends, religious institutions, schools, life experiences, the mass media, and interest groups. As Americans read less, television and radio talk shows and Internet chat rooms are helping shape public opinion in the way that newspapers once did. In a large and diverse state such as California, organized interest groups and the enormous number of media outlets available have become vital components of the political process.

THE MASS MEDIA: A MASSIVE INFLUENCE

Perhaps nothing better illustrates the power of the media to influence politics than the election of political newcomer Arnold Schwarzenegger as governor of California. Although he had no experience in office, his years starring as "the Terminator," who could solve problems with brute strength, apparently gave many California voters a sense of confidence in his political problem-solving ability. Entertainment merged with news coverage as the Schwarzenegger campaign caravan rolled through the state during the recall of 2003.

Fascination with "Arnold" created a brief media focus on state politics, but the broadcast media soon returned to its habits of occasional coverage of our state capitol. Most broadcast media (television and radio) focus on national and international news, or churn out coverage of "news lite" stories of crime, freeway chases, and natural disasters. For many years, only those willing to make time to read newspapers could find out anything about state or local politics. Newspapers still provide more in-depth coverage of issues, and those with computer access can get news from the Internet. (See Appendix C for useful websites.) Since few political candidates begin their electoral careers with the kind of recognition Governor Schwarzenegger had, most politicians must spend vast sums on mass media in order to create a successful political image.

Image making is an expensive and essential business in California. The 2006 state election cost over $600 million for all candidates,[1] and no candidate for any office is considered "serious" by media or voters unless he or she has sufficient financial resources to run. Campaign funds are spent on various forms of communication, including television, radio, mailings, telephone calls, e-mail, and person-to-person precinct walks, all of which are coordinated by high-cost campaign consultants. The larger the electoral district, the less likely a campaign will include any personal contact but rather will depend on mail and media. Critics charge that political information conveyed by the media emphasizes personality factors, attacks, and scandals rather than significant policy issues, but despite "peace pledges" and other gimmicks, most candidates eventually use negative campaigning to attract voter attention.

ECONOMIC INTEREST GROUPS: PRESSURE WHERE IT COUNTS

Organized *interest groups*—also known as lobbies—are also important in shaping public opinion and have been unusually influential in California politics. These groups often spend money through their *political action committees (PACs)*, which raise money to be spent on campaign contributions. Interest groups aid individual candidates by providing them with publicity, financial contributions, and campaign workers. The most powerful groups are usually those with the most financial resources, including the majority of business interests and some of the larger unions, such as those for public school teachers and state prison guards. When a group supports a successful candidate, it then gains better access to that politician than most other individuals ever have. Lobbies spend more money in California than in any other state, with over $212 million in 2004.[2]

Interest groups generally avoid direct affiliation with any political party, preferring instead to work with whichever politician is in office.

<table>
<tr><td colspan="3">**TABLE 5.1**</td></tr>
</table>

Political Contributions to State-Level Candidates, 2002

Sector	Amount Contributed	Number of Contributions
Unknown (individual relatives, friends, etc.)	$60,495,242	76,356
Finance, insurance, real estate	$44,841,466	25,348
Labor unions	$39,505,907	11,161
Political parties	$27,645,211	6,190
Other/retiree/civil servants	$19,077,273	34,142
General business	$17,255,968	17,347
Candidates (to themselves and others)	$16,712,308	729
Communications, media, and electronics	$16,277,794	6,561
Health industries/professionals	$15,580,436	15,692
Construction	$9,062,665	8,647
Agriculture, food distributors	$6,597,324	6,048
Energy and natural resources	$5,592,477	3,906
Transportation, tourism	$4,174,508	2,714
Ideology/single issue	$1,709,950	620
TOTAL CONTRIBUTIONS FROM ALL SOURCES	**$305,788,486**	

Business vs. Labor Totals for 2002

Sector	Amount Contributed	Number of Contributions
All business	$121,927,563	81,088
Labor (public and private sector)	$39,505,907	11,161

Top Donors in Selected Categories

Sector	Contributor	Amount Contributed
Ideology/single issues	Christian Conservative	$551,000
Non-California entities	Tribal Governments	$6,019,180
Entertainment/tourism	Beer, Wine, and Liquor	$3,818,293
Labor unions	Public Sector Unions	$20,639,776

Source: National Institute on Money in State Politics: Follow the Money, www.followthemoney.org.

Business groups usually prefer to help elect Republicans, whereas labor groups prefer Democrats. The influence of various interest groups is indicated, in part, by their wealth and the number of people who belong to or are employed by their organizations. Nearly all of California's most profitable corporations, including oil companies, insurance giants, utilities, banks, and telecommunications companies, are linked together in pressure groups such as the California Manufacturers and Technology Association, the Western States Petroleum Association, and the California Cable and Telecommunications Association.[3] Other major *private-sector* players in the lobbying game are the California Nations Indian Gaming Association, the California Association of Realtors, the California Medical Association, the Trial Lawyers Association, and the Agricultural Producers. The California Teachers Association, the California Correctional Peace Officers Association, the California State Employees Association, the California Labor Federation, and many other groups represent labor interests, though not necessarily in a unified manner. Labor groups, particularly public employee unions, worked in unity to defeat all the ballot measures in Governor Schwarzenegger's unpopular 2005 special election, leaving the governor to admit that "I learned my lesson."

Repeated attempts to curb the spending and influence of special interests have had limited success. Under the "free speech" rights guaranteed by the U.S. Constitution, courts have repeatedly ruled that limits on campaign contributions are a limit on free speech. This enables large organizations as well as affluent individuals to continue dominating campaign fund-raising. Californians may be dismayed by the role of huge campaign dollars, but they have not figured out how to end this.

OTHER INTEREST GROUPS: LESS MONEY BUT STILL A VOICE

In addition to the business, professional, and labor groups that spend money to elect candidates and later make contact with elected officials to share their views, California's political process has enabled less affluent interest groups to develop and participate. Such groups, discussed in the next chapter, include those representing various ethnic communities, environmental organizations such as the Planning and Conservation League, Children Now (which concerns itself with the needs of youth), and single-issue groups such as the California Abortion Rights Action League, Handgun Control, the Fund for Animals, and Surfriders (whose primary interest is in protecting beaches). These groups may not provide much campaign funding, but they often offer volunteers whose election support activities gain credibility for the organization.

In addition to an enormous array of nongovernmental lobbies, government agencies also lobby for their concerns, with numerous cities, counties, and *special districts*, such as water agencies and school districts, employing paid lobbyists in Sacramento. These government entities often seek funding or other legislative support from the state.

LOBBYISTS IN ACTION: A HIGH-SKILL, HIGH-PAY CAREER

The term *lobbying* arose when those who wanted to influence elected officials would congregate in the lobbies of government buildings and wait to speak with a politician about their concerns. California's lobbyists, like those around the nation, gradually developed a pattern of wining and dining the politicians as well as giving them gifts and campaign contributions. Periodic *scandals* in which lobbyists and legislators are convicted of crimes involving trading votes for financial rewards create public demand for reform of the lobbying industry. The 1974 Political Reform Initiative requires each lobbyist to file monthly reports showing income, expenditures, and steps taken to influence government action. This initiative also created the Fair Political Practices Commission (FPPC), which oversees campaigns and lobbying and monitors any possible wrongdoing by candidates or PACs. The computer-literate person now has more opportunity to track political finances as a result of the Online Disclosure Act (1997), which requires all lobbying expenditures to be posted online at http://cal-access.ss.ca.gov (a site located within the secretary of state's website).

The most recent effort to control campaign spending was Proposition 34 (November 2000). This ballot measure was written and passed by the legislature and then approved by voters. Many political experts question whether the provisions are strict enough and criticize the measure for leaving too many loopholes for wealthy special interests. Meanwhile, the size of average contributions to state Assembly and Senate campaigns increased by one-third.[4] Proposition 34 does not control spending by "independent expenditure campaigns," in which special-interest groups run ads and send mailers without coordinating their effort with the candidate.

In addition to helping favorable politicians get elected, lobbyists perform an assortment of tasks to achieve their organization's goals. Many lobbyists are former lawmakers or legislative aides, whose personal contacts enable them to work successfully in the halls of power. They earn substantial salaries for handling the following:

1. Campaign efforts (primarily financial contributions) to elect sympathetic candidates, especially incumbents.
2. Testimony for or against bills being considered by legislative committees.

3. Informal contacts with lawmakers for purposes of providing them with information, statistical data, and expert opinions on pending legislation.

4. Ads and announcements in newspapers, on websites, and through direct mail, which appeal to the public to take a position and convey their views to elected officials.

5. Sponsorship of initiative or referendum petitions to put propositions on the ballot for the approval of the voters.

6. Encouragement of interest group members to write letters to lawmakers regarding particular bills.

7. Organization of protest marches and other forms of public demonstrations.

8. Favorable publicity and endorsements for cooperative lawmakers inserted in the internal publications of the organization.

9. Attempts to influence the appointment (by the governor) of sympathetic judges and administrative officials.

With the passage of *term limits* (Proposition 140) in 1990, the influence of lobbyists has changed. Before term limits, lobbyists could develop ongoing friendships with legislators, who often spent decades in office. Now, legislators rotate out of office frequently, and lobbyists must quickly develop relationships with newly elected officials and their new staff members. Those newly elected officials may be more susceptible to lobbyists, because lobbyists have much more experience in Sacramento than most new legislators.

Because lobbying still determines the outcome of almost all legislation, Californians who realize how much political decisions can affect their daily lives usually become interested in tracking the impact of lobbying on their elected officials. This involves checking campaign donation records as well as legislators' voting records in order to find out how a particular group has influenced a specific legislator. Two excellent sources of information are the secretary of state's Cal-Access website and www.followthemoney.org. The best solution for individuals interested in more direct involvement may be to join the interest groups that reflect their values and political concerns. Many lobbies are open groups that welcome new members. These include organizations involved with environmental issues, ethnic concerns, health care, and many more. (See Appendix A for a directory of organizations anyone can join.) Members receive updates from lobbyists indicating what legislation is being considered and how the individual can phone or write in a timely, informed manner. (See Appendix D for information about contacting elected officials.) Any individual Californian can write a letter, but the most effective political action comes through organized groups.

QUESTIONS TO CONSIDER

Using Your Text and Your Own Experiences

1. In how many ways do mass media influence political attitudes? Give examples of those influences. Remember that media include both the information media and the entertainment media.

2. What makes a special-interest group powerful? Are there problems with how much power some of these groups have?

3. Is personal wealth an essential ingredient for individual political influence? If you are not wealthy, what can you do to have a voice in California's political process?

ENDNOTES

1. National Institute on Money in State Politics, http://www. followthemoney.org.

2. Jamie Court, "Sacramento's Scandal-in-waiting," *Los Angeles Times,* 24 January 2006, p. B13.

3. "Top 10 Lobbyist Employers Ranked from High to Low," 1 January 1999–30 September 1999, Secretary of State 3rd Quarter Report, http://www.ss.ca.gov.

4. Raymond J. La Raja and Dorie Apollonio, "Term Limits Affect Legislators' Fund Raising Prowess," Institute of Governmental Studies Public Affairs Report, University of California, Vol. 40, No. 5, September 1999, p. 3.

CHAPTER SIX

Political Parties and Other Voluntary Organizations

"The success of the Republican and Democratic parties is gauged by how they do at election time; electing their candidates is their primary focus."

—Ken deBow and John Syer, political scientists

Although most Californians who are registered voters belong to one of the two major parties, a substantial minority have chosen other voting affiliations. Over 18 percent of California voters belong to no party ("decline to state" or "unaffiliated" registration status), and another 4 percent are members of one of the five minor parties, with these numbers increasing each year.[1] Many citizen activists remain almost entirely separate from party organizations and yet are immersed in the *grassroots* political process through an enormous variety of voluntary associations, some of which, like many Parent Teacher Associations (PTAs), Neighborhood Councils, and homeowner groups, have become highly politicized. Activities that used to require volunteers with time and energy and little political awareness now require participants who understand the intimate links between one's neighborhood problems or local school issues and the larger California political and budget process. Parents of children in dilapidated schools, homeowners concerned about graffiti, and beach lovers whose shores are polluted are among many Californians whose political involvement begins when they collect signatures for ballot initiatives or lobby public officials in an effort to resolve their particular problems.

Meanwhile, despite the small numbers of Californians who participate directly in their political parties or feel any special enthusiasm for either party, *party affiliations* are reflected in the voting patterns of legislators and the track records of governors. On many issues of major public concern, such as traffic and transportation, criminal justice, the environment, and funding for education, the votes of individual legislators may depend more on party allegiance than on any other factor.

DO PARTIES MATTER? THE VOTERS' PERSPECTIVE

California's tradition of minimal loyalty to either of the two major parties has roots in the state constitution's rules regarding state employment and elections. California's *civil service system* fills 98 percent of all state government jobs on the basis of competitive exams, thereby reducing the number of jobs that can be used as *patronage* to reward supporters of the winning party. Local offices (including city, county, and education boards) and all judicial elections are *nonpartisan*, with candidates listed by name and occupation, with no mention of party affiliation. The ballot format itself, known as the *office-block ballot*, lists candidates under the heading of the office being contested rather than in columns divided according to party, and thus encourages voters to concentrate on individual candidates rather than voting a straight party ticket. The nonpartisan nature of most California politics is best understood in terms of the fact that only 179 of the 19,279 elective offices throughout the state are *partisan*.[2]

Although the parties are not as well organized or as meaningful to voters as they are in some other states, Californians display some partisan loyalty. Many voters registered in a party still vote for their party's candidates without much thought, and the enormous amounts of campaign funds spent on media are often aimed at the 22% of voters who are not registered with either major party and therefore are considered "up for grabs" or *swing votes*. Table 6.1 shows historic declines in voter affiliation with the two major parties.

Although voters are less tied to parties than in the past, party leaders and elected officials can be intensely partisan, as exemplified by the annual state budget battles between Sacramento's "Dems" and "Reps." Differences between Democrats and Republicans show up very clearly on matters such as taxation, aid to low-income Californians, and other major fiscal concerns. In principle, most Republicans favor constant tax cuts for business and the upper middle class, whereas Democrats are willing to maintain tax rates to support public education and social programs. Even as the two parties have their differences, the differences

TABLE 6.1

California Voter Registration Patterns, 1950–2006

	Democrat	*Republican*	*Other*	*Decline to State*
1950	58%	35%	1%	4%
1960	57%	38%	1%	3%
1970	55%	39%	2%	4%
1980	53%	34%	3%	9%
1990	49%	39%	3%	9%
2000	46%	35%	5%	14%
2006	43%	35%	4%	18%

Source: California Secretary of State.

within them are perhaps equally important. Moderate Republicans are under severe pressure from the "Christian right" to adopt its antiabortion, antigay rights policies, while mainstream Democrats are reminded by their more liberal colleagues to support gay rights, gun control, and environmental protection.

With all the internal and interparty dissension, it is perhaps no wonder that many citizens register their disapproval by refusing to vote at all or by registering to vote without affiliating with either major party. In the 2006 gubernatorial election, less than 50 percent of registered voters bothered to vote.[3]

MINOR PARTIES: ALTERNATIVE POLITICAL VOICES

Although the state constitution makes it very difficult for minor parties to get on the ballot, California voters manage to show their frustration with the two major parties in other, diverse ways. Between 1966 and 2006, the percentage of voters registered as either Democrats or Republicans dropped from 94 percent to 78 percent.[4] Among the other party options are the Libertarian (belief in *minimalist* government), American Independent (anti-immigration), Greens (environmental focus), and Peace and Freedom (left of center). To attain *ballot status* these parties must get 1 percent of registered voters to write in the new party in the "Other" space on the voter registration form or get 1 percent of voters to sign petitions. They remain official parties with ballot status as long as any of their candidates for statewide office receive 2 percent of the vote.

Then there is the small minority of Californians who belong to the category "Other" and have identified themselves as members of parties known as "Halloween," "Let's Have a," "Utopian Immoralist," "Smash the State," "Marijuana," and numerous other inventive titles.[5] These highly individualized "parties" have little impact separately, but the five official minor parties occasionally pull enough votes away from a major-party candidate to cause an electoral surprise or *upset*.

PARTY ORGANIZATION: WHO MAKES THE RULES?

California's parties are regulated by both state law and their own internal guidelines. The two major parties have identical general structures: a state central committee and 58 *county committees*. The most powerful nonelected official in each party is the state party chair, although this individual is rarely well known by the general public. Beyond these two committees, much of party organization is left to each party. Democrats have organized themselves into Assembly district committees, whereas Republicans rely primarily on county committees for their local activities. (See Figure 6.1.) These activities include recruiting candidates, raising money, registering voters, and supporting party nominees in general elections.

This level of political activity involves only a small fraction of the population. Of the 20 million Californians eligible to vote, only 70 percent register, and even fewer actually vote. California utilizes the *semi-open partisan primary*, which allows "decline to state" voters (now 18% of the electorate) to choose a party and request its candidate list for that primary, while party members get only their party's ballot choices.

Even before voter registration in the two major parties dropped to its current low (80% of registered voters), California's parties were designed to be weak. In order to overcome the structural "antiparty" bias of the state constitution, the two major parties attempt to create stronger internal structures by promoting clubs or caucuses. The Republican Party's very conservative Young Americans for Freedom (YAF) claims to "hold the reigns of power" in the party,[6] while the moderate and well-financed Republicans for a New Majority claim increasing influence. Democrats stay close to their liberal roots through the California Democratic Council, the party's largest club. Other small groupings include the Log Cabin Club (Republican gay rights group) and the Democrats for Neighborhood Action (a Los Angeles-based group that has helped elect numerous officials). In general, these internal organizations have only an indirect impact on the larger political process.

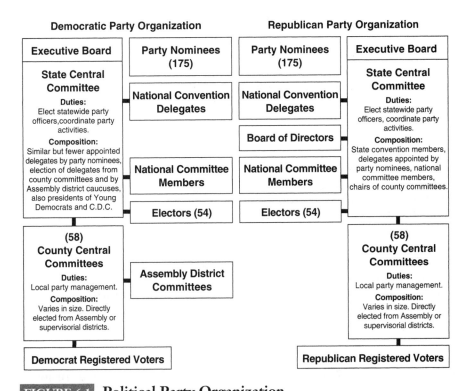

FIGURE 6.1 Political Party Organization

Source: California Government and Politics Annual.

Perhaps because parties are not very powerful, and because most party activists are unknown and unrecognized, many Californians choose to be active politically without being involved in parties.

OUTSIDE PARTIES: NONPARTISAN POLITICAL ORGANIZATIONS

Outside the party structure and party-oriented organizations are the multitude of grassroots groupings that are the actual political focus of many Californians. Perhaps the growing popularity of such groups reflects the historical weakness of parties and the current low profiles of the partisan organizations. Or perhaps the issues that confront Californians daily are best approached through issue-oriented organizations with no absolute loyalty to any party.

For those concerned with environmental protection, groups such as Save Our Coast (based in San Mateo), the Labor/Community Strategy Center (in Los Angeles), the League of Conservation Voters (statewide), and numerous other local and regional groups are in constant need of volunteers' time, energy, and money. For women seeking greater representation, the California chapters of the National Women's Political Caucus, the California Abortion Rights Action League, and the Los Angeles-based Fund for a Feminist Majority all raise money and organize volunteers to get women into office as well as to elect men sympathetic to feminist concerns.

African-American and Latino activists are often involved in California affiliates of the Southern Christian Leadership Conference, the National Association for the Advancement of Colored People, the Southwest Voter Registration and Education Project, the Mexican American Political Association, and the Mexican American Legal Defense and Education Fund, all of which encourage minority involvement in both electoral politics and community issues. Asian-Americans, rivaling Latinos as the fastest-growing minority group, derive much of their political clout from the Asian Pacific American Legal Center and the Asian Pacific Policy Institute, both in Southern California. All of these groups concern themselves with the ongoing issues of minorities, including access to employment, education, and housing, as well as adequate representation in politics and media.

Other forms of voluntary associations that bring people together include the Bus Riders Union (supporting low-cost transportation), Californians for Pesticide Reform, local homeowner and resident associations, Neighborhood Councils, and numerous ad hoc committees that come together for short-term purposes, such as planting trees or preventing unwanted development projects. California's organized historic preservationists battle to protect architectural and cultural landmarks from demolition, while Neighborhood Watch committees, formed by small groups of neighbors in coordination with local police departments, carry out important tasks such as painting out graffiti, reporting abandoned cars, and keeping track of crime. Voluntary groups whose issues become the focus of widespread concern can ultimately create major changes, such as the "Three Strikes, You're Out" laws that exist in part owing to the political organizing done by families damaged by violent crime.

Californians in search of the California Dream have two clear options: they can "cocoon" themselves into the privacy of their homes and try to block out the social stresses around them, or they can join other concerned people to work toward improving the quality of life. Literally hundreds of organizations exist through the volunteer efforts of people who want to make a difference. The only limits on political participation are the time and energy of people, who may find that their "voluntary" political participation soon begins to feel "essential." Once the connections between individual problems and the political process are made, it becomes difficult to return to a narrow, nonpolitical life.

QUESTIONS TO CONSIDER

Using Your Text and Your Own Experiences

1. What are some issues in everyday life that are impacted by political decision makers? Discuss the importance of understanding this connection between daily life and politics.

2. How important are political parties? Why is there an increase in people registering under "decline to state" or in a minor party? What other type of organization can people join to express their political concerns?

3. Research the current minor parties, their philosophies and their leaders. Can you create the framework for another party that should exist in California?

ENDNOTES

1. Secretary of State Voter Registration Data, 10 February 2003, http://www.ss.ca.gov/elections/elections_u.htm.
2. David G. Savage, "Nonpartisan Vote Challenge Voided," *Los Angeles Times,* 18 June 1991, p. A3.
3. Mark Z. Barabak, "Negative Campaign Repelled Some Voters," *Los Angeles Times,* 11 November 2002, p. B1; Kristen Walbolt, "How California Voted," *Los Angeles Times,* 9 October 2003, p. A24.
4. David Lesher, "California: The Decline to State," *California Journal,* February 2002, p. 8.
5. Ray Reynolds, *California the Curious* (Berkeley Bear Flag Books, 1989), p. 168.
6. Bud Lembke, "Pulse Beats," in *Political Pulse,* quoting California Young Americans for Freedom newsletter, 27 August 1999, p. 6.

CHAPTER SEVEN

Campaigns and Elections: Too Many?

"Money is the mother's milk of politics."
—Former California Assembly Speaker Jess Unruh

Public officials are normally chosen in a two-step process involving both primary and runoff or general elections. California's state primaries, usually in June, are *semi-open*, in which party members get their party's list of candidates, and "decline to state" voters (who do not belong to any party) may choose a "party for today's primary" and vote in the primary of one of the state's official parties. Since many "decline to state" voters do not know they can vote in partisan primaries, they often fail to turn out to vote, therefore missing their chance to vote on the nonpartisan local races or ballot propositions that may be on the same ballot.

Any registered voter may run for an office in the primary by filing a declaration of candidacy with the county clerk at least 69 days before the election, paying a filing fee (unless granted an exemption based on inability to pay), and submitting a petition with the signatures of from 20 to 500 registered voters, depending on the office sought.

In a partisan primary designed to select party candidates, the party nomination is won by the candidate with the *plurality* of votes. In a nonpartisan contest, such as for county supervisor, one candidate must get a true *majority* (50% plus one) in order to win. Therefore, if no candidate in the nonpartisan primary receives a majority, the two with the most votes face one another in a later *runoff election*. Nonpartisan elections are held for city, county, judicial, and local education offices (school boards, community college boards).

In general elections, held in early November of even-numbered years for state and national offices, the ballot includes the nominees from each party for each office and all propositions that have qualified for that ballot. Most voters still go to the *polls* to vote, but an increasing number take advantage of *vote-by-mail* ballots to vote at home and mail their ballots, thus saving the time it may take to vote in person. Anyone may request a mail-in ballot, and increasing numbers of voters are using this convenient method of participating in elections.

CALIFORNIA POLITICIANS: SEE HOW THEY RUN

It is relatively easy to run for office in California, but to win requires a combination of campaign ingredients that may be difficult to assemble. One of the most important is an "electable" candidate. Name recognition is important, and the occasional political success of a well-known actor always reminds us that voters like to vote for familiar names, and not necessarily on the basis of political background or qualifications.

Familiar political names can also develop in ambitious families. In Los Angeles, there is the Hahn family (father Kenny was a county supervisor, son Jim was mayor, and daughter Janice is on the city council), and in the Inland Empire, there is the Calderon family, with brothers Tom, Ron, and Charles all serving in the legislature at various times. Similarly, the widows of elected officials are often chosen to replace their husbands, in part because of name recognition. Both Mary Bono (R, Palm Springs) and Lois Capps (D, Santa Barbara) were elected to complete the congressional terms of their deceased husbands and were then reelected on their own in subsequent years. And California is home to the first "sister team" in Congress, Loretta and Linda Sanchez, both of whom serve Southern California districts.

MONEY AND POLITICS: THE VITAL LINK

In part because name recognition is so important, and because it takes a lot of money to create that recognition, California campaigns are now so expensive that one of the greatest dangers to democratic politics is that races are often won by the biggest spenders, not necessarily the best candidates. Until recently, *incumbents* typically had the advantage in terms of finances and name recognition, but both *term limits* and the recent trend toward extremely wealthy individuals spending millions to create name identification have altered the situation. Open races in which there is no incumbent sometimes result in a more level playing field for candidates;

however, wealthy individuals can buy name recognition by spending enormous sums of their personal funds on media and mailers.

Both incumbents and *challengers* channel many of their campaign dollars to highly paid consultants, who push their clients to raise even more money in order to pay other campaign costs. Much of the money is spent on broadcast media, especially radio and television ads. The increasing use of the Internet to promote campaigns is relatively inexpensive but still reaches only the techno-literate population, and most campaign strategists do not rely on the web to mount a successful campaign. Although TV ads are not efficient because they reach so many nonvoters, they are still essential components of most statewide campaigns and, for local races, may utilize local cable channels to target voters.

Every election season, the amount of money that politicians spend on campaigns could cover the costs of some of the most needed services in the state. Each election sets new records for campaign spending, with the 2005 special election costing special interests over $500 million, without counting the public taxpayer cost of $50 million for the ballots, pollworkers, and other costs in each county. For eight ballot measures, all of which lost, and no candidates, this was perhaps California's most costly election. Many police officers, teachers, firefighters, and mental health workers in the state would gladly have seen those same hundreds of millions spent on the services they strive to provide. Despite periodic voter-approved campaign reforms, money is still the major factor in most elections.

In addition to broadcast media purchases, campaign costs include various consultants' fees, polling costs, and direct mail to voters. Direct mail has become an intricate business in which experts help candidates mail persuasive literature to *target audiences.* In tight races, where *swing voters* may make the difference, one brochure targets conservatives while another appeals to liberals. Another frequent strategy is to avoid mentioning party affiliation in order to appeal to the many Californians who are registered as *decline to state.* Like other Americans, Californians turn out to vote in proportion to the amount of media attention and controversy generated by an election as well as in relation to how "turned off" they are by negative campaign tactics. Some candidates benefit from a small turnout and help create that outcome by using ads that are intentionally ugly.

The millions of campaign dollars come from a variety of sources. The Fair Political Practices Commission, set up by voters in 1974 through the initiative process, keeps records of donations. The pattern of donations continues to show high spending by special-interest groups, which now also benefit from their own independent-expenditure campaigns, in which they promote candidates or ballot measures separately from the official campaigns. Top campaign spenders include virtually the same list of pressure groups that also lobby Sacramento throughout the year: oil companies, utilities, tribal gaming, telecommunications businesses, banks, agribusinesses, insurance corporations, doctors, lawyers, labor unions, teachers, and prison guards. Political fund-raisers report that an average of 85 percent of the money raised for candidates is "the cost of doing business" for special-interest groups, with the remaining 15 percent being "love money" from friends and family.[1]

Although most campaigning is done with dollars, California voters occasionally get a taste of the more personal campaign styles of the past. During election season, those who are registered to vote may answer the doorbell and find a campaign staff member or volunteer coming to chat. Occasionally, the candidate actually visits in person; however, only a candidate who is very dedicated or reasonably well-to-do can afford to quit work to campaign on a daily basis. Automated phone calls or calls made by volunteers are also used, with calls placed to those whose voting record indicates they are "likely to vote."

ELECTIONS WITHOUT CANDIDATES: DIRECT DEMOCRACY

Our federal system is a *representative democracy* in which voters elect officials to make decisions for them. The federal system has no form of direct citizen decision making: every decision is made by elected officials. However, states may choose to develop their own forms of *direct democracy,* in which voters may bypass elected officials to make laws themselves or even to remove elected officials from office. California's direct democracy was created by the Progressives of the early 1900s as part of their strategy to bring political power back to the people, and Californians have made ample use of this opportunity. California's constitution ensures that the state's voters can make laws, amend the state constitution, repeal laws, or recall elected officials through the ballot box.

The most commonly used of the three forms of direct democracy—the initiative, referendum, and recall—is the *initiative.* (See Figure 7.1.) The initiative permits registered voters to place a proposed law, or *statute,* on the ballot through petition signatures equal to 5 percent of the votes cast in the last election for governor (the current required number of valid signatures is 375,000). Similarly, voters may propose amendments to the state constitution (which requires 8 percent to get onto the ballot, or 600,000 signatures). Petition circulators are given 150 days in which to gather signatures. The secretary of state receives the petitions and evaluates whether enough valid signatures have been collected. If there are enough signatures, the measure is given a proposition number and can be approved by a simple majority in the next election. Because of the high costs of qualifying an initiative and promoting its passage, the large majority of initiatives on the ballot are written and promoted by

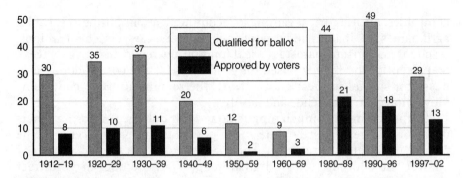

FIGURE 7.1   **California Initiatives, 1912–2002**

organized special-interest groups, which usually pay professional signature gatherers to qualify propositions to appear on the ballot.

Less frequently used are *referendums*, of which there are two types. One type allows voters to repeal a law passed by the legislature. Owing to the requirement that all signatures must be gathered within a mere 90 days of the legislation's passage, this type of referendum has rarely appeared on the ballot. The second type of referendum is one submitted to the voters by the legislature rather than by petition; this is most frequently used for *bond measures*.

The third component of direct democracy, the *recall*, is a device by which voters can petition for a special election to remove an official from office before his or her term has expired. Unlike impeachment, which is initiated by the elected legislative body, recall efforts begin with petitions by registered voters (often mobilized by a special-interest group's dollars). Recall attempts are more common than actual recall elections: prior to 2003, there were 35 recall efforts against California governors, but none obtained enough signatures to get on the ballot. Then the recall drive against Gray Davis, fueled largely by Republican Darryl Issa's millions, obtained the required 900,000 signatures and thus succeeded in getting onto the ballot. A recall petition normally requires the valid signatures of 12 to 25 percent of those who voted in the last election; if that requirement is met, anyone may file to run for that office. Voters must then vote on whether or not to recall the official and on which of the other candidates to elect to fill the possible vacancy. There can be no runoff; the candidate with the most votes wins the position.

DIRECT DEMOCRACY: PROS AND CONS

The Progressives intended that the initiative, referendum, and recall would help citizens make policy directly or remove incompetent officials, thus counteracting the corruption of state or local officials who might be too subservient to powerful special interests. Instead, those same special interests have grown sophisticated in their use of these mechanisms to achieve their goals. Because the signatures of about 420,000 registered voters are necessary to place a statutory initiative on the ballot (and over 670,000 are required for a constitutional amendment) and because signature gatherers must get twice as many as required in order to offset the many invalid signatures found by the secretary of state, it can easily require over $1 million just to qualify a measure. The costs to publicize the measure (by those favoring and those opposing it) can go into the multimillion-dollar range—just for one controversial proposition. Another problem is that there are no limits on the number of propositions per election—voters may become overwhelmed by the work required to read and evaluate dozens of ballot measures. Yet another problem with initiatives is that measures may pass by large margins and yet still have unconstitutional elements which the courts then negate. As to the recall, critics suggest that it can be used unfairly against a competent but unpopular official.

Most political experts and politicians believe that California's direct democracy needs reform. Ideas for improvement include imposing a legal review of propositions before they are circulated for signatures, changing the time limits for signature gathering, making it easier for the legislature to amend initiatives without returning to the voters, and enforcing the requirement that initiatives deal with only one subject.

Perhaps one reason that it is so difficult to reform the direct democracy process is that it still serves one function: to remove power from elected officials and grant that power to the voters. In some sense, direct democracy adds a fourth element to the checks and balances of the three branches of government, one in which the voters themselves find a voice— a voice that may differ enormously from the ones emanating from the halls of government in California.

CLEANING UP POLITICS: CAMPAIGN REFORM

Every few years yet another "campaign reform" initiative seems to appear on the California ballot. Often, two conflicting initiatives may deal with the same issue. Over time, voters have approved restrictions on transfers of funds between candidates, required reporting of donations to the Fair Political Practices Commission, and imposed strict limits on the amount a lobbyist can spend to "wine and dine" an elected official. Yet it seems that each time voters say yes to a reform, the unintended consequences of the law show up in later years and demonstrate the difficulty of separating money from politics. The most recent effort, the California Clean Money Initiative, which would have created public financing, was defeated by voters after corporate interests spent millions to oppose it.

TABLE 7.1

Voter Ethnicity in General Elections

Year	Latino	White	Asian	Black	Other
2000	14%	71%	6%	7%	2%
1998	14	74	4	7	1
1996	12	76	4	6	1
1994	9	77	4	8	2
1992	8	79	4	7	2
1990	4	82	4	8	2

Source: *California Journal*, September 2002.

THE CHANGING ELECTORATE: WHO VOTES AND WHO DOESN'T

With about one-quarter of the population being immigrants from other nations,[2] California's pool of eligible voters is proportionately smaller than that in many other states. Traditionally, voter turnout in California is similar to that in other states: many fewer people vote than are eligible. Nonvoters include the "contented apathetics," who just aren't interested in politics because they see no need to be; people who are devoting all their time to economic survival and don't have time or energy to become informed citizens; and those who are "politically alienated" and believe their vote makes no difference.[3] Voters tend to be affluent, educated, and older than average, leaving many younger, poorer, and less educated Californians underrepresented in the electoral process. In California, the electorate is much "whiter" than the population, with about 70 percent of voters being white, even though whites make up somewhat less than half the population. (See Table 7.1.) Until ethnic minorities and lower-income citizens vote in larger numbers, the trend toward a multicultural state with a *monocultural electorate* will continue.

Having a real democracy requires time and energy from ordinary citizens. Otherwise, the few who bother to vote will exercise disproportionate power, and those they elect may feel responsible to fewer people rather than to society as a whole.

QUESTIONS TO CONSIDER

Using Your Text and Your Own Experiences

1. Discuss the relationship between money and politics. What forms of political activity and access are available to people who do not have large sums to give to candidates or PACs?

2. Debate the pros and cons of our three direct democracy mechanisms. Would California be better off without them or with a modified version?

3. Take a class survey. Pair up voters with nonvoters to discuss the issue of voter participation. Does your classroom reflect the mono-cultural electorate or a changing electorate? Can voters persuade nonvoters to use their franchise?

ENDNOTES

1. Interview with Pat Bradford of Bradford and Rix, 15 August 2003.
2. U.S. Census Bureau.
3. Richard Zeiger, quoting Mervin Field, "Few Citizens Make Decisions for Everyone," *California Journal*, November 1990, p. 519.

CHAPTER EIGHT

The California Legislature

"I came up here to be a legislator, which I thought was like being an intellectual in action. What I found was I was an assembly worker in a bill factory."

    —Former Senator Tom Hayden (D, Santa Monica)

The California legislative branch is a bicameral body consisting of a 40-member Senate elected for a four-year term and an 80-member Assembly elected for a two-year term. Half of the Senate and the entire Assembly are elected in November of even-numbered years.

Each Senate district must be equal in population to all other Senate districts, with the same rule holding for all Assembly districts. Thus, each Senate district includes twice as many residents as each Assembly district, and state senators are considered more powerful than Assembly members. Each Senate district includes two Assembly districts. (See Figure 8.1.)

THE STATE OF THE LEGISLATURE: CHAOS IN MOTION?

Like many political bodies in the United States, California's legislature often ranks low in public support. While overt corruption (such as taking campaign contributions in direct exchange for a specific vote) is rarely discovered or publicized, partisan battles and resulting inaction can destroy public confidence. The legislature consistently receives low rankings in public support, yet California's legislators have one of the nation's best pay and benefit packages, with salaries of $110,880 per year, plus generous expense accounts. Perhaps it is no wonder that furious voters approved Proposition 140 (1990), which demanded strict term limits for legislators and executive-branch officials and also eliminated the legislators' state-funded pension plan.[1]

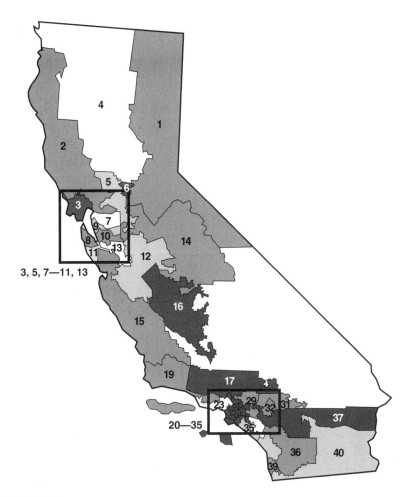

FIGURE 8.1 **Senate Districts**
Source: California Journal.

However, voters may not have realized the full impact of their term-limit decision. Along with the six-year limit on Assembly service and the eight-year limit on senators, the proposition cut legislative budgets in ways that led to the loss of many highly skilled legislative staff members. Rapid turnover in elected legislators and the relative inexperience of their staff members actually give more power to the over one thousand registered lobbyists[2] using their unlimited years of experience to influence the rookie legislators. Nor have term limits ended political ambition: many legislators now recycle themselves by running for local offices after they are "termed out."

Despite all these shortcomings, Proposition 140 has brought new faces to Sacramento and has increased the ethnic and occupational diversity of our legislature. Those who worry that the quality of the legislature is diminished by the constant turnover have proposed that the limits be increased to 12 years per house (with an individual eligible for a total of 24 years if he or she wins a full measure of Assembly and Senate terms). Thus far, this change has proven too controversial to be enacted.

REDISTRICTING AND GERRYMANDERING: DRAWING THE LINES FOR WINNERS

Because legislators run from specific, numbered districts (80 Assembly and 40 state Senate), voter registration numbers in each district essentially determine which party will hold the legislative seat. District boundaries are redrawn every ten years (after each U.S. Census), in a process known as *redistricting*. Lines for the state Assembly and Senate are decided by the legislators, who depend on highly skilled demographers and political scientists to assist them. The legislature also has the responsibility to redraw California's 53 congressional districts. Redistricting traditionally involves a manipulation of boundaries (known as *gerrymandering*) primarily to maintain the strength of whichever party has a majority in the legislature. Gerrymandering is highly political and has been blamed for the strong ideological divide in the legislature, in which Democrats tend to be very liberal and Republicans very conservative, with little room for moderation or compromise.

Criticism of the partisan gerrymander, which currently favors Democrats, has led to numerous efforts to take redistricting from the legislature and have retired judges perform this task. Thus far, no such change has been authorized by voters, and *safe districts* now dominate the process so much that the Democratic majorities (25 to 15 in the Senate; 48 to 32 in the Assembly) have changed little over several decades. In safe districts, one of the two major parties has such a strong majority of registered voters that their candidate is sure to win in November. Thus, the dominant party's June primary becomes the real battleground, and more "extreme" candidates tend to win primaries, since voter turnout is smaller and more likely to reflect the extremes in the party.

LEGISLATIVE FUNCTIONS AND PROCEDURES: HOW THEY DO THEIR BUSINESS

Unlike the U.S. Congress, which has complete legislative power in the national government, the California legislature must share lawmaking authority with the voters through the initiative and referendum processes described earlier. However, most state laws are determined in Sacramento. In addition, the legislature has the "power of the purse," levying taxes and appropriating money to finance the operation of all state agencies. After passage of Proposition 13 in June 1978, the legislature provided a large percentage of local government revenue as well.

The legislature meets in two-year sessions. A bill introduced during the first year may continue to be considered during the second year without being reintroduced. When a bill is introduced, it moves slowly (with rare exceptions) through a complex process of committee hearings until it reaches the floor of the house where it began. Every bill must go through at least one committee, pass the full house, move through the second house's committee and floor, and then, finally, be sent to the governor. During this process, most bills are *amended*, in part owing to the extensive lobbying by special interests affected by the legislation's intent.

The powers of the Senate and Assembly are nearly identical, although only the approval of the Senate is needed to confirm certain administrative appointments by the governor. A member of either house can introduce any bill, and a majority of the entire membership of both houses is needed to pass most legislation. Figure 8.2

Initial Steps by Author

Idea
Suggestions for legislation come from citizens, lobbyists, legislators, businesses, governor, and other public or private agencies.

Drafting
Formal copy of bill and brief summary are prepared by the legislative counsel.

Introduction
Bill is submitted by senator or Assembly member, numbered and read for the first time; Rules Committee assigns bill to a committee. Printed. Action in house of origin.

Action in House of Origin

Committee
Once in committee, testimony is taken from author, proponents, and opponents. Bills can be passed, amended, held (killed), referred to another committee, or sent to interim study. Bills with a fiscal impact are referred to Appropriations Committee (Senate) and Ways and Means (Assembly).

Second Reading
Bills that pass out of committee are read a second time and placed on file for debate.

Floor Debate and Vote
Bills are read a third time and debated. A rollcall vote follows. For ordinary bills, a majority is needed to pass. For urgency bills and appropriation measures, a two-thirds majority is needed. Any member may seek reconsideration and another vote. If passed, the bill is sent to the second house.

FIGURE 8.2 **How a Bill Becomes Law in California**
Source: Los Angeles County Almanac, 1991.

Disposition in Second House

Reading
Bill is read for the first time and referred to a committee by the Assembly or Senate Rules Committee.

Committee
Procedures and possible actions are identical to those in the first house.

Second Reading
If approved, the bill is read a second time and placed on the daily file for debate and vote.

Floor Debate and Vote
As in the house of origin, recorded votes are taken after debate. If the bill is passed without having been further amended, it is sent to the governor's desk. (Resolutions are sent to the secretary of state.) If amended in the second house and passed, the measure returns to the house of origin for consideration of amendments.

Resolution of Two-House Differences

Concurrence
The house of origin decides whether to accept the other house's amendments. If approved, the bill is sent to the governor. If rejected, the bill is placed in the hands of a conference committee composed of three senators and three Assembly members.

Conference
If the conferees fail to agree, the bill dies. If the conferees present a recommendation for compromise (called a conference report), both houses vote on the report. If the report is adopted by both, the bill goes to the governor. If either house rejects the report, a second conference committee can be formed.

Role of the Governor

Sign or Veto?
Within 12 days after receiving a bill, the governor can sign it into law, allow it to become law without his signature, or veto it. A vetoed bill returns to the house of origin for possible vote on overriding the veto (requires a two-thirds majority of both houses). Urgency measures become effective immediately after signing. Others usually take effect the following January 1st.

FIGURE 8.2   (continued)

shows the procedure followed when a bill is introduced. A two-thirds majority is required for budget bills, proposed constitutional amendments, *overrides* of a veto, and urgency measures, which, unlike most laws, take effect immediately rather than on January 1 of the following year.

PRESIDING OFFICERS: EACH PARTY
GETS SOMETHING

The lieutenant governor is the presiding officer, or president, of the Senate. In that capacity, however, he or she has little power and can vote only in cases of a tie. The person with greatest influence in the Senate is usually the *president pro tem* ("for a time"), a senator who is elected as a substitute presiding officer by the entire Senate and automatically becomes the chair of the powerful Senate Rules Committee. The pro tem is almost always a member of the party with a majority of senators. To counterbalance the pro tem's power, the minority caucus selects a minority leader to organize its work.

Like the Senate president pro tem, the speaker of the Assembly is elected by the entire body and is typically a member of the majority party. The speaker is supposed to preside over the assembly but often delegates the actual task to a speaker pro tem while the speaker "works the floor" (walks around lobbying the members). Once the most powerful legislator, the speaker's role has diminished since term limits make longevity in this role impossible. The minority party caucus elects its own floor leader as well as caucus chair.

COMMITTEES: WHERE THE REAL
WORK GETS DONE

As in Congress, all members of the legislature serve on at least one *standing committee*. Most members of the Assembly serve on three committees, and most senators on four or five. (Table 8.1 lists standing committees of the state Senate during 2002–2003.) Each bill that is introduced is referred to the appropriate committee and is considered by it in an order usually determined by the chairperson. Most bills that fail to become law are killed in committee; those enacted have often been amended there before being considered on the floor of the Senate or Assembly, where they may be further amended.

In contrast to the situation in the U.S. Congress, committee chairs in the state legislature are not determined by seniority. In the Senate, the power to organize committees and appoint their chairs and members is vested in the Rules Committee, made up of the president pro tem and four other senators (two from each caucus). In addition to the Rules Committee, among the most important are the Education, Budget and Fiscal Review, Revenue and Taxation, Transportation and Housing, and Health committees.

In the Assembly, the speaker assigns most committees except for the Rules Committee. Among the most powerful is the Appropriations Committee, which, like the Senate Budget and Fiscal Review Committee, considers all bills that involve state spending. Other important Assembly

TABLE 8.1

State Senate Standing Committees, 2005–2006

Agriculture
Appropriations
Banking, Finance, and Insurance
Budget and Fiscal Review
Business, Professions, and Economic Development
Education
Elections, Reapportionment, and Constitutional
    Amendments
Energy, Utilities, and Communications
Environmental Quality
Governmental Organization
Government Modernization, Efficiency, and
    Accountability
Health
Human Services
Judiciary
Labor and Industrial Relations
Local Government
Natural Resources and Water
Public Employment and Retirement
Public Safety
Revenue and Taxation
Rules
Transportation and Housing
Veterans Affairs

Source: California State Senate.

committees are the Insurance, Education, Agriculture, and Banking and Finance committees.

If either house adds an amendment to a bill that is unacceptable to the house that first passed it, a *conference committee* consisting of three senators and three Assembly members attempts to reach a compromise acceptable to both houses. When a bill is finally passed in the same form by both houses, it is sent to the governor for final action.

LOYALTIES IN THE LEGISLATURE: PARTY, PUBLIC, OR PERSONAL?

Does the state legislature serve itself, the parties, or the public? In terms of public services, a critical issue is the state of the economy. During prosperous times when people are employed and spending money, tax

Recent Laws Created by Our State Legislature and Signed by the Governor: (These are just a few of the 780 laws passed in 2005.)

Environmental Laws:
AB 1125, Pavley, D-Agoura: Requires stores that sell rechargeable batteries to take them back for recycling.
AB 405, Montanez, D-San Fernando: Prohbits use of certain pesticides on school premises.
AB AB 515, Richmand, R-Northridge: Allows private companies to lease space for solar panels along State Water Project.

Animal Laws:
SB 1028, Bowen, D-Marina del Rey: Outlaws remote killing of animals over the Internet and any business that offers shooting of live animals online.
SB 914, Kehoe, D-San Diego: Makes it an infraction punishable by $250 fine to sell a puppy under eight weeks old without written approval from a veterinarian.

Laws Affecting Minors:
AB 1474, Maze, R-Visalia: Drivers under 18 may not drive between 11 P.M. and 5 A.M. for the first year they hold a license.
AB 2943, Pavley, D-Agoura: Chidren under 3 may not get vaccinations that contain a certain quantity of mercury.
AB 646, Runner, R-Lancaster: Makes it an infraction, punishable by $250 fine, to pierce the body of a minor without written consent of parent or guardian.

Privacy issues:
SB 833, Bowen, D- Marina del Rey: Bans sending junk faxes from California and allows people receiving them to sue senders.
SB 355, Murray, D-Culver City: Imposes Penalties up to $2500 for using e-mail to deceive people into releasing private information that can be used for fraud.
AB 381, Montanez, D- San Fernando: Permits lawsuits against paparazzi who commit assault in order to obtain a photograph or recording.

Various:
SB 565, Migden, D-San Francisco: Allows domestic partners to transfer property to each other without triggering reassessment and taxation at current value.
SB 644 Ortiz, D-Sacramento: Requires pharmacists to fill prescriptions, such as for contraceptives, even if they have personal moral objections.
SB 897, Scott, D-Altadena: Extends law allowing California to create trade office in the Republic of Armenia, based on private donations.

revenues are high, and legislators can decide how to spend state money with reasonable amicability. Both parties can look good to their constituents when money flows well. When the state is underfunded, bitter battles erupt between the two parties about how to provide services without adequate funds. On nonbudget matters, such as gay marriage or driving laws for minors, political philosophy and lobbying input will influence lawmakers' decisions. Personal style and political experience also have some impact. When moderate individuals become legislative leaders, they seek to reduce tensions between individuals and parties and to achieve compromise. But owing to term limits, legislators and their leaders rotate out quickly, and many inexperienced lawmakers often do not know the path to compromise. Heavily gerrymandered districts also tend to elect extreme candidates, not moderates, thus adding to the partisan battles. This kind of internal strife often contributes to the public's sense that the elected officials are not putting public well-being first.

Although legislators are often criticized for placing petty concerns above public well-being, the legislature as a body will continue to pass thousands of bills that, if signed by the governor, can affect all Californians. See Table 8.2 for recent laws passed by the state legislature and now in effect in California.

QUESTIONS TO CONSIDER

Using Your Text and Your Own Experiences

1. Define *redistricting* and *gerrymandering*. How do the two concepts relate? Which word is more realistic to describe the process of redrawing political boundaries? Why?

2. What is your impression of California's legislative system? Is it efficient? Is it responsive to the public? How could the legislative process be improved?

3. How have term limits affected California's lawmaking process? Why do most lawmakers oppose term limits? What do you think of term limits?

ENDNOTES

1. Interview with Mike Ward, Budget Officer of the California State Senate, 8 August 2000.
2. Jamie Court, "Sacramento Scandal-in-Waiting," *Los Angeles Times*, 24 January 2006, p. B13.

CHAPTER NINE

California's Plural Executive: Governor Plus Seven

"When the Legislature and the governor work together to solve people's problems, the voters stand with us."
—Fabian Nunez, Speaker of the Assembly, Nov. 7, 2006.

California's governor, former actor and bodybuilder Arnold Schwarzenegger, is one of the most powerful people in the nation, with powers including spearheading the annual budget process, appointing numerous executive and judicial officers, signing or vetoing legislation, deciding clemency for convicted criminals, and many ceremonial activities.

VETO, BUDGET, APPOINTMENTS: THE TOP POWERS

When the legislature passes a bill, the governor has 12 days in which to *veto* it by sending it back to the legislature or to sign it into law. If he or she does neither, the bill becomes law automatically. The only time a governor gets more time is when the legislature goes into recess or adjourns and hundreds of bills may arrive in a few days. In this situation, the governor has 30 days to make decisions about bills. Governors vary in their eagerness to veto, and the frequency of the veto depends in part on whether the governor and the legislative majority are from the same party. If the legislative majority is from the other party, the governor may be sent many bills that are sure to be vetoed because of partisan conflicts or ideological differences. Only rarely can the legislature amass the two-thirds vote necessary to *override* a veto, so the governor's veto is a very powerful tool.

The budget powers begin with a ceremonial moment: every January 10th, the governor presents a budget proposal to the legislature for the fiscal year starting July 1st. Although the bill may be much amended before it is passed and returned to the governor in June, he or she may then use the *item veto*. This permits the deletion of a particular expenditure entirely or the reduction of its amount, thereby giving the governor major control over state spending, from start to finish. Appointment powers include giving positions both in the judicial branch and in the executive bureaucracy (see Figure 9.1) The people given these high-level jobs can shape the effectiveness of our courts as well as numerous state agencies.

OTHER POWERS: NEW IDEAS AND "LIFE OR DEATH" CHOICES

The governor's other powers include various "checks and balances" with the legislative and judicial branches. For the legislature, the governor's powers include sending messages to suggest new legislation and the authority to call special sessions. Ideas for new laws are often announced in the annual State of the State speech which is usually given along with the budget proposal. Concepts presented here can then be introduced as bills into the state Assembly or Senate by the governor's allies in those bodies. In addition, the governor can call a special election, regardless of any opposition to this costly action.

Perhaps the governor's most emotionally difficult power is *executive clemency*, which consists of pardons, commutations (reductions of sentences), and reprieves (postponements of sentences) granted to convicts. Governors may grant a life sentence instead of execution to those already handed a death sentence by a jury and court, and some of these cases (such as the Tookie Williams execution in 2005) attract international attention.

UNUSUAL CIRCUMSTANCES: MILITARY AND POLICE POWERS

The governor, as commander-in-chief of the California National Guard, may call the guard into active duty for in-state emergencies. Because the National Guard can also be called to duty by the president for national service, many California National Guard members are now serving in Iraq. The governor may also direct the California Highway Patrol to bolster

TABLE 9.1

Checks and Balances:
The Governor's Appointments

Vacant Position	*Who Must Confirm Governor's Candidate*
Judicial: Appeals courts and state Supreme Court	Commission on Judicial Appointments
Judicial: Superior courts	No one (valid until next scheduled election)
U.S. Senate	No one (valid until next scheduled election)
County supervisor	No one (valid until next scheduled election)
Governor's personal staff	No one
Governor's cabinet	State Senate
Executive departments	State Senate
Boards and commissions	State Senate
Constitutional officers	State Senate and Assembly
Board of Equalization	State Senate and Assembly

local police and sheriff's officers if intervention is needed on a smaller scale. Generally, governors hope that California remains free of earthquakes, floods, major fires, or riots during their term of office, thus avoiding any need to use these powers.

APPOINTMENT POWERS: JOBS AT THE TOP

The governor enforces state laws through a vast administrative bureaucracy consisting of about 50 departments, most of which are currently grouped within five huge agencies: Business, Transportation and Housing, Health and Welfare Resources, State and Consumer Services, and Youth and Adult Corrections. (See Figure 9.1.) The heads of these agencies, in addition to the directors of the Departments of Finance, Food and Agriculture, Industrial Relations, Trade and Commerce, Environmental Protection, Child Development and Education, and the Director of Information Technology, constitute the governor's cabinet and are appointed by the governor, subject to Senate confirmation. The finance director is responsible for preparing the entire state budget for submission to the legislature. In keeping with California's tradition of mistrust of political patronage, the governor actually appoints only 1 percent of the total state workforce, with the remaining state employees being civil

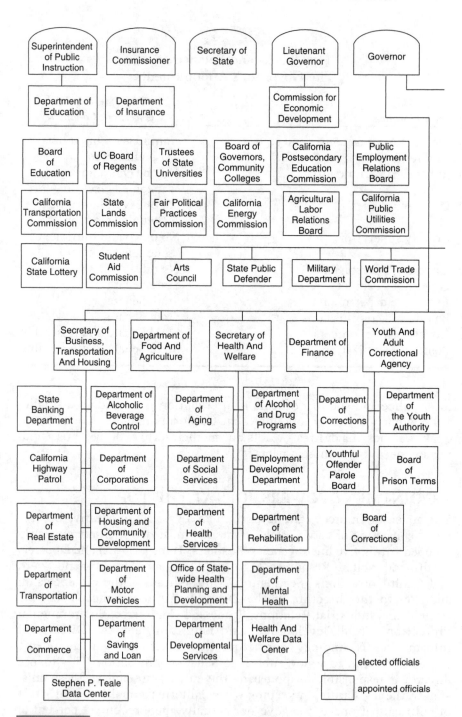

FIGURE 9.1 **California State Government: The Executive Branch**
Source: League of Women Voters.

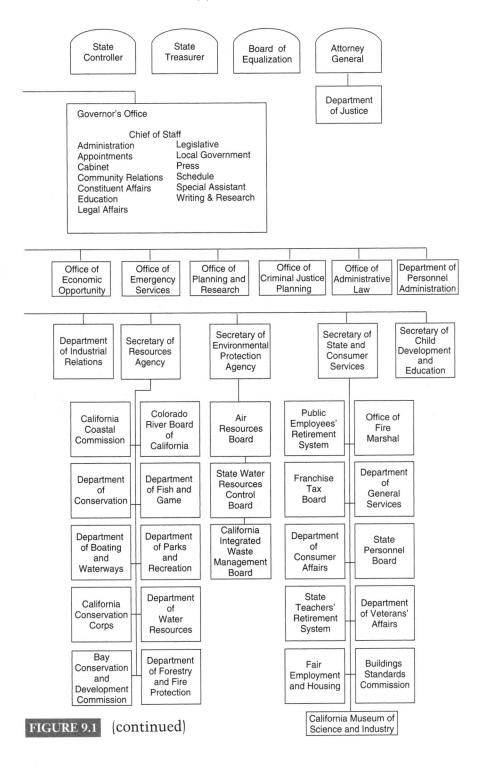

FIGURE 9.1 (continued)

servants.[1] However, those several hundred appointed jobs are at the highest levels of government and determine the functioning of virtually every state-run operation.

The governor also has the power to appoint members of many administrative boards, four of which are in the field of education. Most appointments are made with the concurrence of the state Senate, and appointees are usually political supporters of the governor. Among these are the following:

1. The Board of Regents, which governs the nine campuses of the University of California (UC) and consists of 18 members appointed by the governor for 12-year terms, 7 ex-officio members, and 1 UC student who serves a one-year term.

2. The Board of Trustees of the 20-campus California State University system, composed of 18 gubernatorial appointees who serve eight-year terms and 5 ex-officio members.

3. The Board of Governors of the California Community Colleges, a 16-member group (including 1 faculty and 1 student member) appointed by the governor for four-year terms to coordinate the 72 locally controlled community college districts.

4. The State Board of Education, the ten members of which are appointed for four-year terms to make policy for public schools throughout the state on such matters as curriculum and textbook selection.

5. The five-member state Personnel Board, appointed for ten-year terms, which supervises the civil service system encompassing 98 percent of state employees.

6. The five-person Public Utilities Commission, appointed for six-year terms, which licenses more than 1500 privately owned companies and regulates the rates charged and services provided in the gas, water, telephone, telegraph, electricity, and transportation industries.

7. The five-member Energy Commission, appointed for the purpose of coordinating energy needs and resources as well as promoting conservation and alternative technologies.

8. The seven-member Fair Employment and Housing Commission, with responsibility for enforcing the laws against both job and housing discrimination.

9. The Workers' Compensation Appeals Board, consisting of seven members, which settles disputes regarding money paid to employees suffering job-related injuries or illness.

10. The Board of Prison Terms, whose nine members determine which convicts should be granted parole from state prisons.

11. The five-member Public Employment Relations Board, which regulates collective bargaining involving unions of workers employed by the state government and by public schools, colleges, and universities.

12. The five-member Alcohol Beverage Control Board, which determines what alcohol licenses can be granted throughout the state.

Most governors try to balance political patronage with some semblance of screening for qualifications before they appoint their supporters to government positions. Because most appointments require state Senate approval, the governor's relationship with the majority party in the Senate may determine whether or not appointees are confirmed. The Senate has been known to be very selective, withholding approval of the governor's first choice if the majority party is unhappy with the governor's policies, or if the Senate leaders deem the nominee to be underqualified.

In addition to the many state boards and commissions the governor must fill, he or she also has the authority to appoint replacements to fill vacancies created by death or resignation on county boards of supervisors as well as those occurring for any of the seven other executive officers and for California's U.S. senators. With so many responsibilities, California's governor is certainly comparable in importance to top corporate executives, yet the governor's salary is $175,000 per year, much less than the multimillion-dollar salaries of most corporate leaders.

THE PLURAL EXECUTIVE: TRAINING FOR FUTURE GOVERNORS

In addition to the governor, seven other executive officials are elected directly by the voters. Like the governor, they are chosen for four-year terms (with a limit of two terms) and hold the following positions, often known as *constitutional offices*.

1. The lieutenant governor, in addition to being nominal president of the state Senate, succeeds to the governorship if that office becomes vacant between elections. The lieutenant governor also serves as acting governor when the governor is out of the state. A recall of the governor does not create a vacancy; the process actually includes the selection of a replacement governor, and the office of lieutenant governor is not affected.

   Because of the *office-block ballot*, with its emphasis on voting separately for each state office, Californians have often elected a governor from one party and a lieutenant governor from the other major party. This system, in which the second in command may be from a different party than the governor, has been criticized for promoting inefficiency and poor coordination between public officials. Longtime Democratic politician John Garamendi is the current lieutenant governor.

2. The attorney general, the chief legal adviser to all state agencies, is also head of the state Justice Department, which provides assistance to local law enforcement agencies, represents the state in lawsuits, and exercises supervision over the county district attorneys in their prosecution of state criminal defendants. Democrat Jerry Brown, who has served as governor, is the attorney general.

3. The controller is concerned with government finance. He or she audits state expenditures, supervises financial restrictions on local governments, and influences state tax collections as a member of the Board of Equalization. Moreover, the controller has considerable patronage power in appointing inheritance tax appraisers and is a member of the State Lands Commission, which oversees the state's 4 million acres of public lands. He or she is also chair of the Franchise Tax Board, which collects income taxes. Democrat John Chiang serves as controller.

4. The California secretary of state maintains official custody over state legal documents, grants charters to business corporations, and administers state election procedures. One of the most important tasks of the secretary of state is to verify the signatures on petitions for ballot initiatives, referendums, and recalls, and to administer state election laws. Democrat Debra Bowen is the only woman serving in the plural executive.

5. The state treasurer maintains custody over tax money collected by various state agencies, deposits it in private banks until appropriated by the legislature, sells government bonds (presumably at the lowest possible interest rate), and influences stock investments by the public-employee pension funds. Democrat Bill Lockyer, former attorney general, now serves as treasurer.

6. Until 1988, the insurance commissioner was appointed by the governor. A ballot initiative made the position an elected post. Steve Poizner is the only Republican besides the governor to serve in a constitutional office. His job is to monitor the corporations that sell various types of insurance: life, health, automobile, homeowner, earthquake, and any other forms of insurance sold in the state.

7. The superintendent of public instruction is elected on a nonpartisan basis, unlike the governor and the six executive officers listed above, who are nominated and elected through partisan campaigns. The superintendent directs the state Department of Education and is charged with the responsibility for dispensing financial aid to local school districts, granting teaching credentials, and enforcing policies determined by the state Board of Education. In addition, the superintendent is an *ex-officio* member of the UC Board of Regents and the California State University Board of Trustees. Democrat Jack O'Connell from Santa Barbara was reelected in 2006.

In addition to the constitutional executive officers just mentioned, California voters choose four members of the Board of Equalization from the four districts into which the state is divided for this purpose. This board collects the sales tax, a major source of state revenue, and equalizes the basis on which local property taxes are assessed by the 58 county assessors in California.

Although the executive branch, including its many agencies, appears large and perhaps excessively layered with bureaucracy, California has been cited as the state with "the most efficient use of bureaucrats" because it employs only 5.75 state workers for every 1000 Californians.[2]

Despite this positive assessment of the state's bureaucracy, the election of so many executive officials is frequently criticized. The voters have little information about the candidates seeking these offices, and the governor cannot coordinate their activities effectively. This problem is particularly acute when some of the constitutional officers are not of the governor's party or are even potential future rivals for the governorship. However, despite suggestions from the Constitutional Revision Commission to reduce the number of elected executive officers (and replace them with appointees),[3] there is little indication that the structure at the top will change soon.

QUESTIONS TO CONSIDER

Using Your Text and Your Own Experiences

1. Describe some of the governor's powers. Which ones are most important (i.e., affect large numbers of people and are used frequently)? Which ones does a governor prefer not to use?

2. Discuss the governor's powers to appoint government officials. How does this power help shape the everyday lives of Californians? Give specific examples.

3. What is the relationship between the governor and the legislature? What checks and balances are built into the California constitution for these two branches of government?

ENDNOTES

1. Bradley Inman, "Many Are Calling but Few Will Be Chosen," *Los Angeles Times*, 17 March 1991, p. D2.
2. Dan Miller, "State's Numbers Say It All," *City and State*, 23 April 1990, p. 14.
3. Final Report and Recommendations to the Governor and the Legislature from the Constitutional Revision Commission, Sacramento, 1996, p. 18.

CHAPTER TEN

Paying the Bills: California's Budget Struggles

"Key aspects of the way California collects and apportions tax revenues are greatly flawed. . . . The big losers in California's game of fiscal roulette have been its communities and its people."

—Antonio Villaraigosa, Mayor of Los Angeles[1]

Perhaps the most persistent problem of all governments is finding adequate financial resources to do the many tasks expected of the public sector. Even as people complain incessantly about insufficient levels of service, many of them also fiercely resist being taxed to pay for needed improvements. Such contradictions become even more acute in difficult economic times when unemployment rises (thus reducing the total amount of income tax paid) and the needs for unemployment funds, educational opportunities, or welfare programs increase. In prosperous periods, tax collections generally rise, and politicians are tempted to offer "tax cuts," even though not all public services are fully funded. Whether the economy is booming or in a slump, government has only a few options: raise somebody's taxes, provide fewer services, or borrow money and pay it back (with interest, of course) in the future. Each of these alternatives has its own consequences and costs, and it is the process of making these decisions that becomes the annual state budget battle.

HOW THE BUDGET IS DEVELOPED:
A TWO-YEAR PROCESS

Every January, the governor must present to the legislature a budget plan reflecting the governor's priorities. This budget requires many months of preparation and input from the executive branch's various departments and agencies, under the supervision of the Department of Finance. The budget is based on "guesstimates" of the amount the state will collect in taxes and *baseline budgets* from each of the state agencies, cities, counties, and special districts that rely on the state as their primary source of funds. Baseline (or rollover) budgets essentially assume that an agency needs to continue doing everything it currently does as well as receive some cost-of-living adjustment (COLA) raise from the previous year's budget. Of course, agencies may also ask for new funds to provide additional programs, and the governor may wish to initiate new services or reorganize existing programs.

The governor's budget then is examined by the nonpartisan legislative analyst, who reviews the governor's expenditure requests and revenue projections and provides each legislator with comments. Then the legislature begins public hearings held before five subcommittees in each house. During these hearings, state and local government employees (along with the people they serve) testify about why their particular *appropriations* must be maintained or perhaps expanded. Lobbyists for business interests also register their concerns about any taxation changes that may negatively affect their industries.

It is during these budget hearings that the day dreaded by many Californians arrives: April 15. Once tax day is over, the director of finance knows more clearly how much the state has received in personal income taxes and can reevaluate earlier revenue projections to determine whether or not the original budget is accurate. Based on these revised numbers, the governor submits the "May revise." The legislature again discusses the budget, and a conference committee is formed to develop a joint Senate and Assembly budget plan.

The final budget agreement is supposed to be passed by a two-thirds margin in each house by June 15 and signed by the governor by June 30. (See Table 10.1.) When the economy (and tax collections) are strong, the budget is passed and signed relatively promptly. But during tough times, when Democrats fight to maintain services while Republicans insist on "no new taxes," the budget battle can extend for several months past deadline. Democrats may currently dominate the legislature, but they do not have a full two-thirds of members, so budget passage requires a few Republicans to vote yes. Once the budget bill reaches the governor, the chief executive can then utilize the *item veto* to reduce appropriations or even eliminate whole programs. The legislature rarely has the two-thirds

TABLE 10.1
California Budget Process

Executive Branch		Legislative Branch
Administrative departments prepare budgetary requests.	April	
Agencies prepare preliminary program budgets.	May	
Department of Finance and governor issue policy directions.	July August	
Department of Finance reviews agency proposals.	September October	
Commission on State Finance and experts forecast revenues.	November	
Governor finalizes budget and sends it to the state printing office.	January	
January 10: Governor submits budget to legislature.		Fiscal committee chairs introduce governor's proposal as budget bill.
	February	Legislative analyst studies proposed budget; issues *Analysis of Budget Bill* and *Perspectives and Issues.*
	March	
	April	Assembly and Senate budget subcommittees hold public hearings on assigned sections of the budget.
Department of Finance issues revised forecast of revenues and expenditures.	May	Subcommittees complete action on budget.
		Full budget committees hold hearings and vote. Assembly and Senate pass respective versions of the budget bill.
	June	Conference committee of three Assembly members and three senators agree on a compromise budget bill. June 15: Legislature submits approved budget to governor.
June 30: Governor exercises item veto and signs budget act.	July	Legislature can restore vetoed items by two-thirds vote in each house.

majority to override specific item vetoes, leaving the governor in ultimate control over state spending.

SOURCES OF REVENUE: NEVER ENOUGH

The five major sources of money for the state are:

1. *The general fund,* which includes state income tax, sales taxes, bank and corporation taxes, and interest earned by the state on money not currently in use.
2. *Special funds,* including motor vehicle license and registration fees, gasoline taxes, and portions of the sales, cigarette, and horse-racing taxes that are earmarked for specified purposes.
3. *Bond funds,* requiring voter approval, which are monies borrowed from investors and returned to them with interest in the future.
4. *Federal funds,* including "free" money and some grants that require matching state or local commitments.
5. *Miscellaneous revenues,* such as community college fees and contributions to state pension plans.

Figures 10.1 and 10.2 show state revenues and expenditures, respectively, and Figure 10.3 indicates funding sources for the state infrastructure.

Controversies over these revenue sources are endless. Which taxes should be raised? which lowered? Business interests want to reduce

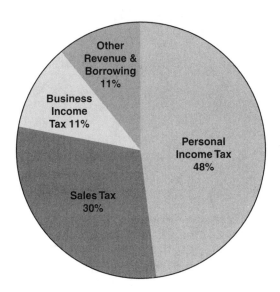

FIGURE 10.1 **State Revenues in 2005–2006**
Source: Legislative Analysts Office.

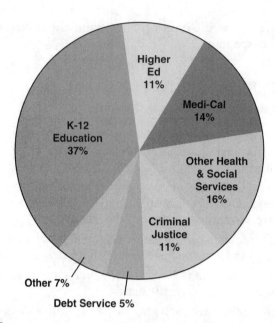

FIGURE 10.2 **Proposed Total State Spending by Major Program Area, 2005–2006**

Source: Legislative Analysts Office.

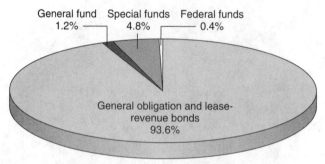

Total 2002–2003 Capital Outlay Funding: $2.2 Billion

FIGURE 10.3 **State Infrastructure Funding Sources (excluding transportation)**

Source: Legislative Analysts Office.

any taxes that cut into their profits, while individuals almost always seem to feel that they are paying too much. The Republican viewpoint has traditionally insisted on reducing taxes regardless of impacts on programs, while Democrats have often proposed closing loopholes that benefit the wealthy in order to protect low-income residents.

Voters are directly involved whenever state or local governments borrow money through *bond issues,* and the historic record suggests that during hard times voters are less likely to approve bonds even though a bond measure may stimulate the economy by creating work for architects, land-use consultants, contractors, construction companies, and so on. All state bonds require only a simple majority, but local bonds now fall into two categories: education bonds require a 55 percent majority, while other local needs (libraries, police and fire bonds, parks, etc.) must still pass with a two-thirds vote. The 55 percent majority for local school and community college bonds has reinvigorated public education as districts throughout California have passed bonds to build new schools and expand colleges. Education bond funds must be used only for land acquisition and buildings; they may not be used for the general operating expenses of the schools or colleges.

VOTER DECISIONS AND STATE FINANCE: DEMOCRACY IN ACTION?

In addition to voting on bond measures, voters have utilized ballot initiatives to make fiscal policy for the state. One of the turning points for California's tax policies was Proposition 13 (June 1978), also known as the Jarvis-Gann initiative in recognition of the efforts of landlord Howard Jarvis and his ally Paul Gann to get the initiative on the ballot. Although its passage occurred over 25 years ago, Proposition 13's causes and consequences are still vital elements in understanding California's situation today.

The roots of Proposition 13 lay in the massive national and international *inflation* of the early 1970s. The causes of the inflationary spiral were primarily outside California, including such factors as heavy federal spending in the 1960s and the oil embargo of the early 1970s nevertheless, these circumstances, added to the traditional speculation in land and property in the state, fueled an enormous rise in the real estate values on which property taxes are levied. Homeowners were suddenly confronted with doubled and tripled *tax assessments* from their county assessor. Faced with the risk of losing their homes, middle- and low-income homeowners gladly joined Jarvis and other major property holders in supporting Proposition 13. When public employees claimed that the proposition would cut not only property taxes on which local governments relied heavily, but also public services, Jarvis replied that "only the fat" would be cut and that the state budget surplus would rescue counties, cities, and school districts if necessary.

These arguments were extremely persuasive—Proposition 13 passed by a landslide, and all property taxes were limited to 1 percent of the assessed value of the property as of 1976, with reassessment to occur only when the property was sold. Since a budget surplus had accumulated in Sacramento, the state did bail out the local governments for several years, but many services were cut back, including library accessibility, fine arts and athletics in the schools, and parks and recreation. In addition, Proposition 13 had some unforeseen long-term impacts, including the shift from local control to a Sacramento-based funding system for cities, counties, and school districts. There were yet other flaws in the measure: notably property owners who rarely sell (such as commercial property owners) experience almost no increase in taxes, whereas owners of individual homes, which are sold more frequently, confront reassessments up to the current market value, causing dramatic tax increases when a home changes hands. Even two neighboring homeowners in identical homes may pay vastly differing property taxes based on when they purchased their homes. This disparity led the U.S. Supreme Court to refer to Proposition 13 as "distasteful and unwise," even as the Court upheld the legality of the law in a 1991 challenge.

During tight economic times, the state's ability to assist local governments is reduced. State budget cuts force cities, counties, schools, and community college districts to go on frequent "begging" expeditions to Sacramento, and in recent years the combined costs of lobbying Sacramento have made local governments, added together, one of the highest-spending lobbying categories.[2]

Through their ballot activism, voters have also placed tight restrictions on the state budget itself. Proposition 98 (1988) requires the state to spend 40 percent of its annual revenue on K–14 education, while another 15 to 20 percent of the budget is set aside to finance bond commitments and voter-mandated programs such as prison construction. Another 25 to 30 percent is mandated by federal law to provide health and welfare assistance, although federal welfare reform does permit the state somewhat more flexibility in how it provides temporary aid to needy families (TANF). Ultimately, the annual budget battle is really a debate about the remaining 15 to 20 percent of the budget pie.[3] (See Figure 10.2 for state expenditures.)

FUTURE PROSPECTS: THE PERMANENT DEBATE

California and its people have ridden a rollercoaster of economic ups and downs since the end of the Cold War (1989–1990). That recession, created mostly by the sudden loss of defense/military jobs, combined with downsizing and mergers in banking and other industries to create a sharp drop in income and sales tax collections. By the mid-1990s, the economy had recovered, especially through the high-tech boom of Silicon Valley's dot.com industry. However, this boom turned into a bust by the year 2000, and the tragedy of September 11, 2001, hurt California's tourism, airlines, and other industries even as the Enron-driven energy crisis ate up billions of dollars. Once again, almost before Californians could fully enjoy their good moment, the economy swooned and the state hit a fiscal crisis. The political strains obviously contributed to the unprecedented ouster of Governor Gray Davis through the state's first gubernatorial recall.

The ongoing unpredictable tides of the global economy, including the impacts of *outsourcing* and *runaway production*, among many factors, continue to cause repeated economic swings from recession to modest recovery. Owing partly to Proposition 13, California relies heavily on volatile income tax revenues, and public opinion surveys indicate voter support for increases in tobacco taxes, Internet taxes, and reforms to Proposition 13.[4] One possible Proposition 13 reform would "split" property tax rolls so that commercial property could be reassessed every ten years and taxed at current value, while maintaining individual homeowners' tax rates for the entire time they own their homes.

During every phase of the state budget cycle, hundreds of groups lobby for their share of revenues while others fight to avoid their share of taxes. Whether or not the economy is strong, everyone wants a piece of the California Dream: schoolchildren and their parents, open-space advocates, prison guards, public employees, library users, college students, welfare (TANF) recipients, automobile users, beachgoers, immigrants, people with disabilities, farmworkers, landowners—the list is endless. For the foreseeable future, California's budget process is bound to be an annual agony that profoundly affects all Californians. Only an informed and politically active public can hope to be considered as elected officials debate the state's budget priorities. Ignoring the process, or the players, may be easy in the short run, but ultimately, we all pay a price if we remain ignorant or uninvolved.

QUESTIONS TO CONSIDER

Using Your Text and Your Own Experiences

1. How does the general economy affect government budgets? What is the role of government in helping the economy grow?

2. Describe the revenue sources and expense patterns of state government. Who benefits from the current structure? Who loses?

3. Evaluate the budget process through its annual cycle. What are some problems with the process? Should anything be changed?

ENDNOTES

1. Honorable Antonio R. Villaraigosa, "A Message from the Speaker," Final Report of the Speaker's Commission on State and Local Government Finance, March 2000, p. 3.
2. Secretary of State, *Lobbying Expenditures and the Top 100 Lobbying Firms*, 1 April–30 June 1994, issued September 1994.
3. "Government in California: Buckling under the Strain," *The Economist*, 13 February 1993, pp. 21–23.
4. Public Policy Institute of California, "State of Change: California 1994–2004, p. 19.

CHAPTER ELEVEN

California Courts and Judges

"Without confidence in a fair and accessible judicial system,
young people are less likely to grow up as law-abiding
citizens."
　　　—Ron George, chief justice of the California state Supreme Court

U nlike the federal system, in which judges are appointed by the president, confirmed by the U.S. Senate, and serve for life with no further review, the state's system involves a complicated combination of appointments and elections for judges. This complex system classifies judges into two categories: trial court judges and appeals judges. The judges and their courts serve the largest population in the nation, cost approximately $2 billion per year to run, and receive nearly two-thirds of that money from the state.[1] They deal with over 8 million civil and criminal cases per year.[2] Like all state-funded systems, the California courts are suffering from budget reductions. The state has more attorneys per person than anywhere else in the world, but the high costs of legal services leave California's 6 million poor people underserved.[3] In addition to legislation, ballot initiatives often determine how courts operate: Proposition 36 (approved by voters in 2000) revised the penalties for drug abuse, replacing jail sentences with drug rehabilitation for many offenders. Additional new programs include the use of mediation rather than court trials to resolve family disputes and other civil matters, and special courts for the homeless.[4]

CALIFORNIA'S TRIAL COURTS: THE FIRST ROUND

California's trial courts (also known as superior courts) handle the first round of both civil and criminal cases. Civil matters include all aspects of family law (divorce, custody, adoption), as well as the many varieties of civil litigation (malpractice, personal injury, bankruptcy, etc.). Criminal trials usually involve misdemeanor and felony charges. Superior court judges earn $127,935 per year and in some counties are assisted by court commissioners who can perform many of the functions of the judges. Courts are organized through counties, with 58 superior court systems ranging from Los Angeles County, which employs hundreds of judges, to Alpine County, with only a few judges.

ALTERNATIVES TO THE COURTS: BUYING JUDICIAL SERVICES

Because of the overcrowded and often delayed court system, Californians, sometimes unwillingly, have turned to private judges to resolve their civil differences. Many Californians do not realize that when they accept many job opportunities or join most health insurance plans, they must sign a binding arbitration clause that denies them the right to sue in court and, instead, requires them to go to binding (no-appeals) arbitration to resolve disputes with the employer or insurer. Private arbitration is different from mediation; mediation is used to resolve issues outside of court, but mediation does not include a "no-appeals" agreement. Private arbitration judges have been criticized for having excessive power, since their decisions are not appealable. There is also some concern that only those who can pay steep fees can afford private judge services. State Supreme Court Chief Justice Ronald M. George has ordered judges to stop working in both arenas and to choose between public judging and private judging in order to avoid any conflicts of interest.[5]

WHERE APPEAL RIGHTS REMAIN INTACT: COURTS IN ACTION

For those who cannot afford or do not wish to use private alternatives, one advantage of using local trial courts to resolve legal problems is the right to appeal. When an individual believes that a lower court has made a legal error in deciding a case, he or she may appeal—if financial resources are available to do so. California is divided into six court of appeal districts, headquartered in San Francisco, Los Angeles, Sacramento, Fresno, San Jose, and San Diego, with a total of 93 judges earning $146,404 each. (See Figure 11.1.) Three judges consider each case primarily by reading transcripts from the original

Supreme Court

1 Chief Justice and 6 Associate Justices

Capital criminal cases*

Courts of Appeal

6 districts, 18 divisions with 93 justices

> **First District**
>
> 4 divisions, 4 justices each; 1 division, 3 justices—
> all in San Francisco = 19

> **Second District**
>
> 6 divisions, 4 justices each in Los Angeles; 1 division,
> 4 justices in Ventura = 28

> **Third District**
>
> 1 division, 10 justices in Sacramento = 10

> **Fourth District**
>
> 1 division, 9 justices in San Diego;
> 1 division, 6 justices in Riverside;
> 1 division, 6 justices in Santa Ana = 21

> **Fifth District**
>
> 1 division, 6 justices in Fresno = 9

> **Sixth District**
>
> 1 division, 6 justices in San Jose = 6

Trial Courts

440 court locations with 1,479 judges;
401 commissioners and referees

Line of Appeal   Line of Discretionary review

FIGURE 11.1 **California Court System** *Death penalty cases are automatically appealed from the superior court directly to the Supreme Court. *Source:* California State Constitution.

trial. The appeals courts continue to see a heavy workload in the areas of juvenile cases, civil cases, and criminal cases.

CALIFORNIA SUPREME COURT: THE LAST RESORT (ALMOST)

Most of the state Supreme Court's work involves handling appeals passed up from the appellate courts. The only cases that come to this court directly are requests from death-row prisoners asking the court to review their sentence. It consists of a chief justice, now Ronald M. George, who receives $163,767, and six associate justices, who earn $156,162. If an individual involved in a case at this level is still not satisfied, he or she may choose to appeal to the U.S. Supreme Court. However, cases that raise constitutional questions appropriate to the U.S. Supreme Court are rare, and the state Supreme Court is the final court of appeal for most cases it determines.

THE SELECTION OF JUDGES: A MIX OF APPOINTMENTS AND ELECTIONS

Every California judge must have worked at least ten years as an attorney in the state, and most attorneys who want to serve as judges also have some form of political connection that puts them on the governor's "short list" for appointment. Although trial court judges are theoretically chosen by the voters in nonpartisan elections for six-year terms, in reality, few judges begin their careers by running for office. When Superior Court judgeships are vacant as a result of death, retirement, or an expansion of the court system, these vacancies are filled by the governor, who has total control of these appointments. Once appointed, the new judge serves until the next election, which is often canceled because no one files to run against the incumbent. Since there are no term limits for judges, those willing to work for public salaries (generally much lower than salaries of private attorneys) can easily sustain a superior court judicial career in California for decades without their names ever appearing on a ballot.

In contrast, for the higher courts, all judges' names eventually appear on the ballot. Appeals court judges and Supreme Court justices are chosen by a method that enhances gubernatorial power to influence the judiciary. The three-step process is as follows.

1. Appointment by the governor based on guidance from his or her judicial appointments secretary.

2. Approval by a majority of the Commission on Judicial Appointments, which consists of the chief justice of the state Supreme Court, the senior presiding justice of the district Court of Appeals, and the state's elected attorney general.

3. Election (confirmation) for a 12-year term, with no opposing candidate permitted to run and voters limited to a choice between yes and no. There are no term limits for any California judges.

In making judicial appointments at all levels, governors usually give special consideration to attorneys who have a good rating from the state Bar Association as well as the right political connections. Like the president, the governor can use judicial appointments to promote his or her agenda. The governor's political views can have an enormous impact on the types of judges appointed. Judicial appointments generally tend to represent the more privileged groups in society (who have the financial resources to become attorneys and the connections to be nominated by the governor) and do not fully reflect the ethnic diversity of California's attorneys. Some governors emphasize the importance of diversity when they appoint judges, while others insist that their selections must be "colorblind." Recent governors, including Gray Davis and Arnold Schwarzenegger, have appointed a fairly balanced group of men and women, Republicans and Democrats.

Once appointed and confirmed, few justices have trouble winning confirmation from the voters. With the unusual exception of the "Dump Rose Bird" campaign of the mid-1980s, neither voters nor election strategists have spent much time worrying about who sits on the California courts. Rose Bird, appointed by Democratic Governor Jerry Brown to the state Supreme Court despite her lack of judicial experience, became the symbol of "soft" liberalism regarding capital punishment. The successful campaign to unseat her also resulted in the voters' removal of two other justices appointed by Democratic governors, allegedly for also being too soft on crime. When these three liberal justices lost their posts, Republican Governor George Deukmejian replaced them with three conservative justices.

Since then, voters have returned to a more normal pattern of confirming gubernatorial appointments and keeping most incumbent judges in office. With rare exceptions, interest in judicial contests is low, and voters often feel that they are casting a ballot blindly when they vote on judges. Few Californians pay attention to the quality of their judges until they need to appear in court and see a judge in action. Like all other elected officials in California, all judges, both trial and appellate, are subject to voter recall, but this process has rarely occurred.

THE NONELECTORAL REMOVAL OF JUDGES: RARE BUT POSSIBLE

Another avenue by which to remove judges is the Commission on Judicial Performance, which can force a judge out even when elected by the voters. The commission includes both judges and nonlawyers appointed by the governor and legislature. Its primary task is to investigate complaints about judicial misconduct and, if circumstances indicate, to recommend that the state Supreme Court remove a judge from office.

The commission receives hundreds of complaints each year about judges. Misconduct charges that may be brought against judges include accusations of racial or gender bias, substance abuse, verbal abuse, accepting bribes, personal favoritism, and even senility. The process of being investigated often results in the voluntary resignation or retirement of the judge in question, thus saving the judge the embarrassment of being forced out of office.

THE JUDICIAL COUNCIL: RUNNING A COMPLEX SYSTEM

The 21 voting members of the Judicial Council are empowered to evaluate and improve the administration of justice in the state. Made up of judges, attorneys, and legislative appointees, the council analyzes the workloads of the courts, recommends reorganizations to improve efficiency, and establishes many of the rules of court procedure. One recent recommendation of the Judicial Council was to update the language used by judges when they give juries instructions so that outdated "legalese" will be replaced by more commonly used terms.[6]

JUDICIAL POWER: WHO HAS IT AND HOW THEY USE IT

While judges at the local level do not permanently affect questions of constitutionality or set policy through their decisions, the appellate justices and state Supreme Court justices can create legal precedents for California through their written decisions. Because these justices wield such power, governors should choose them carefully. However, governors have their own political preferences. They realize that a judgeship will probably last much longer than their term as governor, and they select justices whose overall political views are compatible with their own, expecting these justices to make legal decisions that meet their political goals. Of course, over time, some appointees disappoint the governors who put them there, by making decisions contrary to the wishes of their "patrons."

Six of the seven current members of the state Supreme Court were appointed by Republican governors. Most of them come from a background of business-oriented law, and their rulings reflect those biases.[7] Three of the seven are women, and the court is quite diverse, with a Latino, an Asian-American, and an openly lesbian justice. However, their political views are similar, with most of them being moderate and pragmatic rather than driven by sharp ideological concerns.

Although individuals who have been in California courtrooms and seen judicial authority in action may feel intimidated or powerless, the public must remember that its electoral choice for governor determines the tone of the judicial branch. If one wants liberal judges, one must elect liberal governors, and the same is true for conservatives. If one wants more women and ethnic minorities represented on the bench, one must evaluate the records and promises of gubernatorial candidates regarding judicial appointments. Similarly, if one believes that justice is colorblind, one must try to elect a candidate who promises to select judges without regard to gender or ethnicity. The important element is the citizen's awareness of the connection between voting for governor and the quality of justice in California.

QUESTIONS TO CONSIDER

Using Your Text and Your Own Experiences

1. Compare and contrast the federal judicial system with California's judicial branch in terms of how judges are selected, their length of service, and so on.

2. What is the role of the governor in the judicial branch? Does the governor have too much power? How do voters get involved in judicial selection?

3. Debate the pros and cons of California's judicial confirmation elections. Is judicial independence compromised by this system?

ENDNOTES

1. "Foundations for a New Century," Judicial Council of California, Administrative Office of the Courts, 2000 Court Statistics Report (available at http://www.courtinfo.ca.gov).
2. Ibid.
3. Henry Weinstein, "Legal Aid to the Poor Falls Short," *Los Angeles Times,* 21 November 2002, p. B1.
4. Tony Perry, "Homeless Court Offers New Hope for the Down and Out," *Los Angeles Times,* 22 May 2000, p. A3.
5. Maura Dolan, "Retired Judges Must Choose Between Public, Private Jobs," *Los Angeles Times,* 31 January 2003, p. B1.
6. Jean Guccione, "Relief Coming for Jurors Ill at Ease with Legalese," *Los Angeles Times,* 17 July 2003, p. B1.
7. Bob Egelko, "A Low Profile Court," *California Journal,* June 1994, p. 38.

CHAPTER TWELVE

Criminal Justice and Civil Law

> "We've created 10,000 new jobs in the prison system and
> financed those jobs by cutting 10,000 positions out of the
> university and state college system."
> —Bill Lockyer, attorney general

A ll the vast machinery of the judicial system and its related compo nents, including the judges, attorneys, bailiffs, stenographers, police, jails, wardens, and parole officers (to name a few), serves to facilitate two basic types of legal procedures: civil litigation and criminal prosecutions. Although for many Californians their maximum contact with the entire judicial/legal system is their occasional jury duty, for others their lives are profoundly affected by the structures and processes of the criminal justice system and the civil courts.

CRIMINAL JUSTICE: AN OXYMORON?

Depending on the severity of the act, crimes are normally defined as felonies, misdemeanors, or infractions. *Infractions* are most often violations of traffic laws, whereas *misdemeanors* encompass "less serious" crimes such as shoplifting and public drunkenness. *Felonies*, the most serious crimes and potentially punishable by a year or more in state prison, include both violent and nonviolent crimes.

Like people everywhere, Californians are concerned about protecting themselves from crime. Elaborate alarm systems, gated communities for the wealthy, and a general fear factor permeate daily life. Ballot initiatives such as the "three-strikes" law (1994) created lifetime sentences for a criminal with three felony convictions, but implementation has proven problematic and numerous amendments to that law have been discussed. Despite a huge increase in prison construction and sentencing, crime continues. Except for China and the entire United States, California has the largest penal system in the world. Over 161,000 inmates are housed in 32 prisons, and another 150,000 parolees fall under the Department of Corrections jurisdiction.[1] Many of the prisoners are nonviolent felons whose life sentences cost taxpayers $500,000 to $1 million per inmate.[2] Despite a multimillion-dollar prison construction program, usually in rural locations where prison jobs support the local economy, California's prisons remain tremendously overcrowded, with periodic outbreaks of violence—in some cases involving accusations that prison guards instigated the trouble. Victims of crime are entitled to restitution paid by inmates out of their prison wages and family financial gifts, but many crime victims never receive the funds designated for burials, grief counseling, and lost wages.[3] Table 12.1 lists statistics about the California Department of Corrections.

CRIME AND ITS VICTIMS: TECHNOLOGY ADVANCES, FEARS REMAIN

California crime rates tend to decline during economic good times, but even when employment opportunities are plentiful, not everyone is able or willing to earn an honest living. Those who adopt long-term criminal lifestyles, including drug dealers, gang leaders, and others, may show no interest in "turning over a new leaf" and leaving a life of crime. California has the unhappy role of leading the nation in the growth of youth gangs over the past three decades.[4] Crimes committed by adults are decreasing, while juvenile crime rates continue to increase, fueling concerns that prevention programs involving jobs and education are not funded adequately.[5] Public fears of violent crime have led to a series of ballot initiatives, including Proposition 21 (2000), which requires juveniles aged 14 or older to be tried as adults for murder and which increases penalties for gang-related offenses.

Californians worried about violent crime do not necessarily agree on solutions. While opinion polls repeatedly indicate that a large majority support gun controls, the vocal minority of gun rights supporters continues to lobby against any restrictions. Communities plagued by crime have tried everything from forming Neighborhood Watch committees, which try to link neighbors in a network of alert watchfulness, to demanding speed bumps and private gates. Some local governments have responded by initiating "community policing," a system designed to improve communication between neighborhoods and their police force.[6]

TABLE 12.1

California Department of Corrections, 2003

Budget	$5.237 billion
Portion of state general fund	6.2% (2002–2003)
Average yearly cost	$28,502 per inmate
	$2882 per parolee
Staff	49,570 in institutions, parole supervision, and administration
Facilities	33 state prisons
	38 wilderness area camps
	16 community correctional facilities
	5 prisoner mother facilities
Inmate population	159,390 in all institutions
	94% male, 6% female
	36% Latino, 30% black, 29% white, 5% other
Offense	48% violent crime
	21% property crime
	24% drugs
	7% other
Average reading level	Seventh grade
Special security lifers	25,823
Condemned to death penalty	625
On parole	116,967
Return rate with new prison term	10.6%
Return rate as parole violator	54.2%

Source: California Department of Corrections, www.corr.ca.gov/CommunicationsOffice/facts_figures.asp.

Unfortunately, the responsiveness of government agencies some-times depends on a community's political clout. In low-income areas with little political influence, residents often feel neglected by public safety agencies and do not have the money to purchase alternative sources of protection. More affluent communities have the funds to build gates and walls as well as to hire private security companies to patrol their streets. Underfunding is often blamed for the lack of ade-quate public policing, even while many cities spend millions defending their undertrained law enforcement officers from a variety of lawsuits, including accusations of racial and gender discrimination and various forms of police abuse.

Because most people worry more about violent crime, Californians have just begun to realize the impacts of some new kinds of white-collar crimes. Recent technologies have fueled a stunning rise in identity theft and credit card fraud, while more traditional larcenies continue to cheat ignorant victims through pyramid investment schemes, phony mortgage loans, fraudulent land sales, staged auto accidents, and other illegal and unethical ways to part people from their money. Although most white-collar crime is nonviolent, sometimes auto insurance scam artists cause innocent people to die when they create accidents in order to file personal injury lawsuits. Victims of white-collar crime are often the elderly, immigrants, or the uneducated. Those who use credit cards frequently, especially in gas stations, are also advised to use extra caution against fraud.

The media feed public fears by emphasizing crime as "news," often ignoring more important political news. Since much of violent crime is linked to drug abuse, illegal drug dealing, and domestic violence, the courts are experimenting with "collaborative courts" that involve treatment providers and close monitoring of offenders.[7] Some politicians continue to remind the public that it costs taxpayers about $26,000 per year to keep the average convict in prison,[8] while the state currently spends about $7793 on a public school child and $4500 on a community college student. As a result of the "three strikes" initiative (1994), state prisons are full of aging "lifers" whose medical and other specialized care costs nearly $80,000 per convict per year.[9]

THE CRIMINAL JUSTICE PROCESS: A SYSTEM TO AVOID

In many cases, crimes occur and are not reported, or they are reported but no suspect is arrested. In the cases where an arrest is made, the arresting officer often has the option of "naming" the crime by labeling it either a misdemeanor or a felony. If a person is arrested for a felony, the county district attorney's office must then decide whether to file the felony charge. In cases without witnesses willing to testify, filing charges becomes a questionable proposition in which tax dollars may be spent on a trial only to arrive at an inconclusive outcome. Because of the strength of some gangs, witnesses are often afraid to testify against someone who could take revenge on the witness or a family member.

Under federal constitutional rights, persons accused of crimes are entitled to speedy trials. With the number of felony trials rising 144 percent since 1979,[10] courts must seek ways to reduce their load. *Plea bargains,* in which the accused person's defense attorney can cut a deal with prosecutors and receive a reduced sentence in exchange for eliminating a trial, continue to be common. Defendants with adequate funds may be represented by a private attorney; most accused persons, however, must rely on overworked public defenders to handle their cases. Trials may be decided by either a judge or a jury, depending on the preference of the defendant and his or her attorney. If a jury is used, the entire jury must agree on the final verdict while the judge determines the sentence. The sole exception to this rule is in capital (death penalty) cases, in which the jury, again by unanimous vote, has the duty to recommend either the death penalty or life in prison. (Figure 12.1 shows the locations of prisons in the California system.)

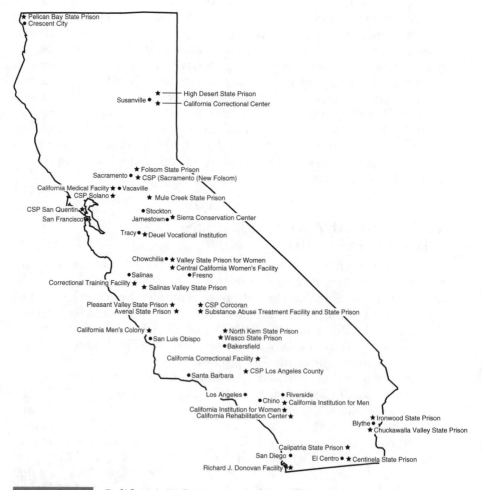

FIGURE 12.1 **California's Correctional Facilities**
Source: California Department of Corrections.

CIVIL LAW: SOLVING PROBLEMS
THROUGH THE COURTS

Whereas criminal law deals with matters that are considered injurious to the "people of the state of California," civil matters involve any disputes between parties which cannot be resolved without legal assistance. Parties involved in such disputes can include individuals, business entities, and government agencies. The range of civil legal matters includes such cases as dissolution of marriage, child custody, personal injury (including automobile accidents), malpractice, workers' compensation, breach of contract, bankruptcy, and many more. In these cases, the court's role frequently is to determine liability and to assess damages, often amounting to millions of dollars.

Most civil lawsuits never reach a court. Those that do go to trial may be decided by a judge or a jury, with only a two-thirds majority of jurors required to agree in order to decide the outcome. Because civil cases have no constitutional protection against delay, waiting for a court date can sometimes last years. One way to avoid the delay is an out-of-court *settlement* arranged by the attorneys of the parties involved. These settlements often save time, money, and aggravation for both the *plaintiff* and the *defendant.* Another alternative to the long wait is to pay private judges to settle disputes outside the public judicial system. Private judges can also prevent public or media access to details about the lives of wealthy or well-known individuals. This *privatization* of the civil legal system may result in speedier justice for those able to buy a judge's time while those involved in the public system continue to wait years for their case to come to court.

JURIES: THE CITIZEN'S DUTY

California has two types of juries: the most common, the trial jury, and the less well-known one, the grand jury. In both cases, jurors must be U.S. citizens. The county grand jury, made up of a select group of citizens nominated by superior court judges, serves a one-year term for minimal compensation, thus leaving this task to the affluent or retired. Their purpose is to investigate possible criminal activity and bring indictments against either public officials or private parties.

Unlike the grand jury which is selected for a year, trial juries are created for the length of a particular trial. For felony trials, the jury consists of 12 citizens, while as few as 9 jurors may try a misdemeanor case or a civil trial. Trial juries are found through both voter registration and motor vehicle license lists. County courts send out notices asking citizens to serve; penalties for failure to respond have increased to $1500 in some counties.

The jury system has been criticized for many reasons, including the low compensation ($15 per day), the potential for emotional (rather than rational) decision making, and the poor use of jurors' time when they do agree to serve. Recent efforts to improve the situation include the one-day-or-one-trial system (which allows people to get back to work more quickly), the use of pager and call-in systems to avoid long waits, and improved jury waiting areas. Although jury duty is often perceived as a boring chore, the jury system is still considered one of the genuine advantages of living in a democratic society with a constitutional right to "an impartial jury" and "due process of law." [11]

QUESTIONS TO CONSIDER

Using Your Text and Your Own Experiences

1. What are some of the root causes of our overloaded criminal justice system? What can be done about solving them?
2. What are some alternatives to our overloaded civil courts? How else can problems be resolved between individuals or organizations?
3. What can be done to increase the number of people who serve on juries? Share your experiences, if any, doing jury duty.

ENDNOTES

1. John Howard, "A New Look at Crime and Punishment," *California Journal,* May 2004, p. 8.
2. Greg Krikorian, "Three Strikes Law Has No Effect, Study Finds," *Los Angeles Times,* 2 March 1999, p. A3.
3. Jennifer Warren, "Victims' Fund May Take More From Inmates," *Los Angeles Times,* 15 January 2003, p. B7.
4. Robert L. Jackson, "California Leads U.S. in Gang Growth," *Los Angeles Times,* 30 May 2001, p. A11.
5. Anne Hendershott, "Juvenile Delinquency and Urban Gangs in California," in Charles F. Hohm, ed., *California's Social Problems* (Addison Wesley Longman, 1997), pp. 99–113.
6. "Community Policing," Huntington Beach Police Department document, Spring 1994.
7. Ronald M. George, Chief Justice of the California Supreme Court, State of the Judiciary Address, 28 March, 2000.
8. California Department of Corrections Facts," 1 August 1997, http://www. cdc.state. ca.us/factsht.html.
9. Sandra Kobrin, "The Price of Punishment," *Los Angeles Times* Magazine, June 26, 2005, p. 10.
10. "Foundations for a New Century," Judicial Council of California, Administrative Office of the Courts, 1999, p. 7.
11. Amendments V and VI, U.S. Constitution.

CHAPTER THIRTEEN

City Governments: Providing the Basics

"The power of local governments to make choices about the level and quality of local services has eroded over the last 20 years. Local communities should be given more local control."

—Constitutional Revision Commission, 1996

There are several types of local government in California—county, city, and special districts—as well as regional agencies that attempt to coordinate their policies. Of these, city government is probably the local government agency that is most accessible to the public. Cities have enormous responsibilities to their residents but are severely constrained by budget limitations, especially the loss of local property tax revenues caused by Proposition 13. As in other levels of government, finding the best ways to generate revenues and provide needed services is an ongoing battle among city officials.

HOW CITIES ARE CREATED: IT'S NOT EASY

With the exceptions of some of the older cities, such as Los Angeles, San Francisco, and San Jose, which received their charters from the state when California was admitted to the Union, mpost cities in California "incorporate" when the residents decide they need their own local government. Before incorporation, areas that are not cities are called *unincorporated areas*, and their residents normally receive basic urban services from the county in which they live. Occasionally, an unincorporated area is simply annexed, or joined with, a nearby city by a majority vote of that territory's residents along with the approval of the adjacent city.

Perhaps the most common reason residents initiate the incorporation process is that the county government, which provides their services, is too far away and unresponsive. If residents believe that police and fire protection is inadequate, or that planning and zoning issues are not well handled, or even that rents are too high in the area, they may organize to create their own city in which they can elect their own officials to control these issues. Of course, residents who want their own city government must realize that there are costs involved in running a city, and they must be prepared to tax themselves to pay for city services. They must also agree to share their tax revenues with the county so it can maintain its countywide services to their residents.[1]

Incorporation begins with a petition signed by at least 25 percent of the registered voters in an area. The petition is then submitted to the Local Agency Formation Commission (LAFCO). Each county has a LAFCO to analyze all issues relating to incorporation, boundary changes, and annexations. The LAFCO must determine the economic feasibility of a proposed city. If the LAFCO decides that cityhood would be financially viable, it authorizes an election in which cityhood can be approved by a simple majority.

CITY RESPONSIBILITIES: MANY TASKS, LIMITED REVENUES

Whether a city is a "general law" city that derives all its powers from statutes passed by the state legislature, or a "charter" city that has its own locally written constitution, all cities share similar tasks and responsibilities. Basic, day-to-day necessities such as sewage and garbage disposal, police and fire protection, libraries, streets and traffic control, recreation and parks facilities, and planning and zoning policy form the backbone of city services. In many cities, some of these services are provided through contracts with the county to purchase services such as law enforcement, fire protection, and street maintenance.

Until 1978, cities obtained about one-fourth of their revenues from local property taxes. After Proposition 13 slashed this source, cities cut back many services and turned to the state capitol in Sacramento for assistance. However, Sacramento does not provide resources comparable to those lost from local property taxes. To fill in the budget gaps, most cities now rely on utility and sales taxes, as well as an array of increased fees, including those for building permits, recreational facilities, real estate transfers, garbage collection, and more. Business licenses, parking taxes, traffic fines, and limited federal grants are additional sources of revenue.

Because sales taxes are often the easiest to collect, city zoning decisions now contribute to "the fiscalization of land use" wherein cities, or their

Community Redevelopment Agencies (CRAs), promote business development at the expense of housing. Neighboring cities fight each other to see which city can offer more financial incentives to the developer of an auto dealer, movie complex, sports arena, or shopping mall, because these land uses will provide sales tax revenue. Rarely do cities offer support for developers of affordable housing, one of the state's most urgent needs. Owing in part to this lack of commitment to housing development, California's housing affordability has fallen into the range where only about one-fourth of Californians can afford to buy the average home, now valued at $319,650.[2]

During a slowdown in the economy, cities, like all government entities, find their tax revenues inadequate for public needs. Police departments usually obtain the largest chunk of city monies, leaving fire services, libraries, parks and recreation, and other departments to battle for their share of the pie.

FORMS OF CITY GOVERNMENT: TWO BASICS WITH VARIATIONS

Although there are numerous local versions, city government in California falls within two broad types. The *mayor–council* variety entails a separation of powers between the mayor, who has executive responsibility for the functioning of most city departments, and the council, which enacts legislation known as *ordinances*. If the mayor has the power to veto ordinances and to appoint department heads, the government is known as a strong mayor–council variety; if not, it is a weak mayor–council system. Larger cities sometimes include aspects of both the strong and weak systems.

The *council–manager* type of government gives the city council both executive and legislative power, but the council exercises its executive power by appointing a professionally trained city manager to coordinate and administer city departments. These city managers are usually very well paid (many earn more than the state's governor) and serve as long as the council wishes. In this form of government, there is a ceremonial mayor with no executive powers who is merely one of the council members. This mayoral position is typically rotated around the council, with each member serving a year and then returning to his or her regular council status. The mayor continues to hold a vote equal to that of every other member of the city council.

Los Angeles and San Francisco employ the mayor–council form, while Oakland, San Jose, and Torrance are among the 90 percent of all cities in the state that use the council–manager form.[3] Under both systems, most cities have a city clerk, attorney, treasurer or controller, and planning commission, with all but the last-named elected directly by voters. The most common departments are police, fire, public works, recreation and parks, and building and zoning. These are usually headed by high-level civil servants or appointees and monitored by advisory commissions appointed by the mayor and/or the council.

While access to city bureaucracies depends in part on the size of the city, a resident with a complaint about city services had best do his or her homework regarding the structure of city government in order to get the fastest and most helpful response. If the bureaucracy that controls the street cleaning services is not responsive, the resident with a dirty street must understand which of the elected officials is most directly responsible for that section of the city in order to obtain better street cleaning. City employees, though generally hardworking and concerned, may go the extra mile if a city council member makes a special request for a constituent. Of course, providing service to individuals can sometimes lead to unethical favors for constituents. If individuals ask for special consideration, such as permission to build larger buildings than current codes permit, outraged citizens may demand investigations of elected officials who try to gain political support through this abuse of power.[4]

CITY POLITICS: POWER BLOCS IN COMPETITION

The forces that influence city politics are even more varied than the forms of city government. Homeowners, builders, city employee unions, historic preservationists, environmentalists, realtors, street vendors, renters, and landlords are among the groups that vie for clout in the city's decision-making process. In city elections, as in most political campaigns, incumbents tend to have the advantage, but an incumbent who has made enough enemies can be ousted by a well-organized challenger. In some cities, term limits have been enacted and opportunities for newcomers have increased. Ironically, despite the many issues determined by city councils, some cities have canceled elections due to incumbents running with no opposition.[5]

One factor in city politics is whether council members are elected *at-large* or *district-based*. In most of California's nearly 500 cities, council members are elected at-large; that is, they may live anywhere in the city. Only a few cities use district-based elections, which divide the city into geographic areas from which council members are elected. (Figure 13.1 shows the 15 city council districts of Los Angeles.) For years, the argument for at-large elections was that the most qualified people could get into office regardless of their address. However, this often results in large sections of cities, particularly those inhabited by ethnic minorities, not being represented on the council owing to the financial advantages of whites from other areas who run for office. In 2000, the U.S. Justice Department sued the city of Santa Paula, alleging that its at-large system prevented Latinos from getting elected.[6] Those who oppose district-based elections

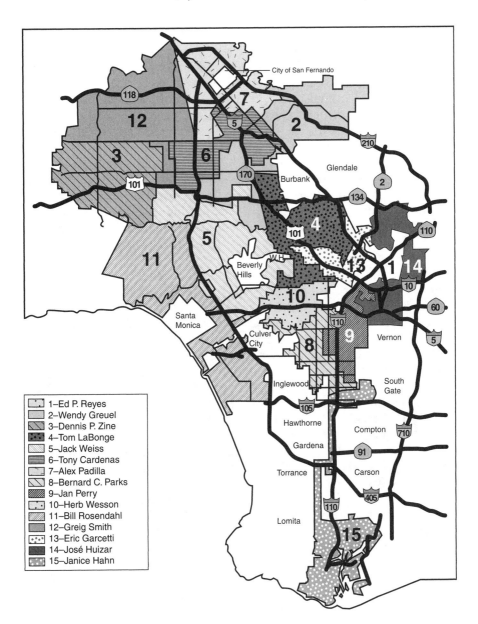

FIGURE 13.1 **Los Angeles City Council Districts**
Source: City Clerk, Los Angeles.

express concerns that districts would lead to *gerrymandering*. Whether under pressure from the federal government or from local residents, most cities that change from at-large to district-based elections usually experience an increase in ethnic diversity on their councils.

Another factor in how well a council represents city residents is whether the council job is full or part time. In most cities, serving on the city council is a form of community volunteerism, with a small stipend paid for countless hours of city-related tasks. In these cases, those able to run and serve as council members tend to be affluent businesspeople or retired persons. In the few cities, such as Los Angeles, that offer full-time jobs to council members, the diversity of professions and backgrounds on the council tends to increase.

In between the four-year election cycle, council business is often handled without much public debate or attention. The battle for power that goes on between elections is most likely to be waged at city council meetings, council committee hearings, or planning commission hearings. Residents affected by a potential ordinance are empowered to speak to the issues before the decision-making body. The Brown Act, or "open meeting law," requires that all local government meetings be open to the public except when personnel matters, legal actions, labor negotiations, or property deals are being discussed. Public notice of meetings and their agendas must be made available in advance, although these notices are often tucked away in little-read newspapers. In some cities, cable television offers residents a chance to see their city council in action.

As in all levels of government, city policies are often determined by those who are most able to contribute to campaigns. It is at the city level, however, that well-organized nonaffluent groups can get involved most successfully. Despite fierce opposition from the business community and the mayor, the Los Angeles City Council was sufficiently influenced by a coalition of city workers and antipoverty advocates to pass a veto-proof Living Wage Act in 1997, which mandates that all organizations with city contracts pay their employees a "living" wage higher than the current minimum wage.[7]

Battles over land use and open space are often fought at the city level as developers run into well-organized opposition from environmentalists, homeowners, and public agencies that believe that more buildings will bring increased demands on public services as well as further deterioration of the natural environment. Battles over large developments on open land often last for decades, such as the battles over the Newhall and Ahmanson Ranches in Southern California, Coyote Valley near San Jose, and the Tejon Ranch in Kern County.

Although many Californians take their city services for granted, the quality of city functions is actually determined by the quality of the elected officials and civil servants of any particular city. Disparities in the quality of these services are part of the reason for the vast differentials in property values around the state. A desirable home is a home in a well-run city, and a well-run city is usually one with large numbers of active community members who demand that public officials be accountable to the people.

QUESTIONS TO CONSIDER

Using Your Text and Your Own Experiences

1. What are the responsibilities of city government? What tax resources can city officials use to accomplish their goals?
2. Compare and contrast the two forms of city government. Which does your city use? What are the pros and cons of each?
3. Discuss the pros and cons of at-large vs. district-based city elections. Which does your city use? Which do you think is best?

ENDNOTES

1. Frank Messina, "Drives Toward Cityhood Slowed by Revenue Law," *Los Angeles Times*, 15 July 1997, p. A13.
2. Lusk Center for Real Estate, University of Southern California, Casden Real Estate Economics Forecast, 2002.
3. Ed Goldman, "Out of the Sandbox: Sacramento City Politics May Go Bigtime," *California Journal*, May 1993, p. 17.
4. Will Rogers, "Intimidation of City Staff Is Rampant, Pair Says," *Glendale NewsPress*, 16 July 1997, p. A1.
5. Douglas P. Shuit, "Lack of Interest Cancels Some Local Elections," *Los Angeles Times*, 21 February 1999, p. A1.
6. Margaret Talev, "U.S. Sues Santa Paula over Voting System," *Los Angeles Times*, 7 April 2000, p. B3.
7. Maryann Mason, "The Living Wage: In the Public Interest?" Chicago Institute on Urban Poverty Paper, 1996.

CHAPTER FOURTEEN

Beyond Cities: Counties, Special Districts, Education Districts, and Regional Agencies

"There is growing recognition that the problems of
metropolitan areas—declining neighborhoods, congested
highways, degraded natural resources—cannot be solved by
individual local governments working alone."

—Myron Orfield, Metropolitan Area Research Corporation

O
f all governmental units, those at the local level are closest to the
people and affect them most personally, through such services as
public safety, traffic regulation, and the operation of public schools. One
might hope, therefore, that they would be the easiest to understand and
control. However, because of the large numbers of local governments
and their confusing and overlapping jurisdictions, this is not the case.
California has a hodge-podge of over 7000 local governments, with a total
of more than 15,000 local elected officials, who often work to provide services duplicated by an agency a few miles away.[1] This chaotic approach to
local governance allows for much "local control," but much confusion
and overlapping as well.

COUNTIES: MISUNDERSTOOD
BUT VITAL ENTITIES

California's 58 counties are administrative subdivisions of the state and run the gamut in geographic size and population. Los Angeles County, with close to 10 million residents, has more people than over 40 states. San Bernardino County, with its 20,000 square miles, is the largest in the country. In contrast, mountainous Alpine County, which borders Nevada near Lake Tahoe, has about 1300 residents, and San Francisco, the only combined city-county in the state, comprises only 49 square miles.

For residents of *unincorporated areas,* counties provide the basic urban services: safety, road repair, zoning, libraries, and parks. Counties also dispense another complete set of services to all residents, both those in cities and those in unincorporated regions. These programs include administration of welfare programs such as Temporary Assistance to Needy Families (TANF); supervision of foster care and adoptions of abused or neglected children; maintenance of property ownership, voter registration, and birth and marriage records; prosecution of felonies; operation of the superior court system; provision of health services (including mental health) to the uninsured; and control of public health problems such as highly contagious diseases and outbreaks of food poisoning.

In order to provide these varied services, counties must receive financial support from the state and federal governments. Nationwide welfare programs such as TANF receive substantial funds from the federal government, while the state provides a large measure of funding for the county's health-care programs and the public protection agencies such as courts, district attorney's offices, and county jails. Like the cities, counties have become heavily dependent on Sacramento since Proposition 13. The state's fiscal crisis puts enormous pressures on counties, and cuts in county health and safety services have impacted virtually every Californian.

In addition to budget constraints, another logistical problem facing California's counties is the overlap of services when cities and counties provide identical services in virtually the same community. County sheriffs' departments continue to serve unincorporated areas just blocks from where those same services are provided by city police departments. Some cities prefer to avoid the costs and liability of running their own police or fire departments and become *contract cities,* which purchase these services from the county.

Another ongoing problem for counties is the issue of adequate representation. With the exception of San Francisco, with its combined city-county status and its 11-member board of supervisors, all counties are governed by five-member boards of supervisors, exercising both legislative and executive powers. In less populated counties, five individuals may be sufficient; in counties such as Los Angeles, five supervisors serving 10 million residents clearly seems insufficient. Despite several efforts to increase the size of the Los Angeles County Board of Supervisors, voters have repeatedly rejected such proposals, primarily fearing greater costs. In addition to electing their supervisors, county voters also usually elect a sheriff, district attorney, and tax assessor.

SPECIAL DISTRICTS: DOING WHAT ONLY THEY CAN DO

Special districts, most of which were created before Proposition 13 altered the state's financial structure, serve the purpose of providing a specific service that no other jurisdiction provides. Special district services include water supplies, street lighting, mosquito abatement, transportation, air quality control, and much more. With over 5000 special districts, California may take the prize for providing local control of services, but the fiscal consequences are high.[2] Normally, each district performs only one task and yet may have a well-paid staff with travel budgets and "perks." Most special districts are governed by the county board of supervisors or their appointees, while some special district boards are elected by the public. Many special district boards operate almost invisibly, making decisions and spending money outside of the awareness of the public or media.

Special districts range in size from small cemetery districts to the Metropolitan Water District of Southern California, which serves six-counties and wields enormous political clout, especially during drought periods, when the politics of water distribution become most tense. Other large special districts include the Los Angeles County Metropolitan Transit Authority and the Bay Area Rapid Transit District. The many special districts, both large and small, create both confusion and costs for Californians. In response to complaints about expensive bureaucracies, the Constitutional Revision Commission has suggested a massive overhaul of special districts,[3] but as yet, no such changes have been implemented.

EDUCATION DISTRICTS: K–12 AND COMMUNITY COLLEGES

Of all the services provided by local governments, the biggest and most expensive is public education. This is the responsibility of more than 1100 education districts, including approximately 630 elementary school districts, 115 high school districts, 72 community college districts, and 285 unified districts providing both elementary and high school programs. These districts each have elected boards, ranging from five to seven members, accountable directly to the voters. Their chief revenue source is the state, with some monies still derived from local property taxes and a tiny portion of their budgets from the state lottery.

California's schools were among the best in the nation until Proposition 13 (1978) drastically cut the primary funding source. (See Figure 14.1.) For the next 20 years, public schools declined in measures such as pupil–teacher ratio, maintenance of school facilities, and number of computers per student. School budgets depend heavily on whether the state economy and budget are flourishing; in recessions, schools and community colleges get cut along with social services and county governments. Compounding the overall issue about inadequate state funding are the enormous differences in quality between affluent, suburban school districts (where property tax revenues are higher and parents can donate more cash) and the schools in most inner cities. School governance itself is an issue because few Californians seem to realize that schools are run by separately elected School Board members; they frequently ask their city mayors or council members to handle education issues, not realizing that a mayor has no direct authority over local schools.

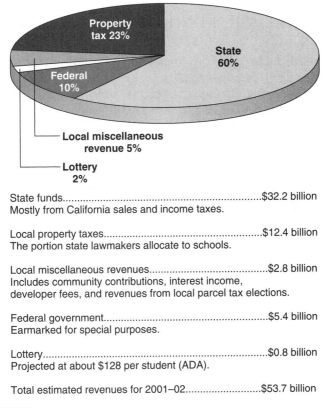

State funds..$32.2 billion
Mostly from California sales and income taxes.

Local property taxes...$12.4 billion
The portion state lawmakers allocate to schools.

Local miscellaneous revenues...$2.8 billion
Includes community contributions, interest income,
developer fees, and revenues from local parcel tax elections.

Federal government...$5.4 billion
Earmarked for special purposes.

Lottery..$0.8 billion
Projected at about $128 per student (ADA).

Total estimated revenues for 2001–02..........................$53.7 billion

FIGURE 14.1 **K–12 Funding, 2000–2001**

Source: California Department of Education, *California Journal.*

Along with the thousand-plus K–12 school districts, 72 community college districts serve the state's adult population. These two-year colleges enable over 1.4 million Californians to earn credits for university transfer, receive vocational training, or learn English as a Second Language and other basic skills. There are no entrance requirements other than being 18 years of age (or, in some cases, being approved to attend at a younger age). Despite substantial fee increases in recent years, California residents still pay lower community college fees than residents of other states, while students from other nations and states pay "out-of-state," tuition which is still considerably less than that of most private colleges. California's community colleges have been hit hard by state budget cuts, and a community college ballot measure has been proposed to stabilize funding and reduce the basic student fee. Though heavily dependent on state funding, each community college district's specific budget decisions are made by a locally elected board of trustees, which also has authority to place bond measures on the ballot for college construction programs.

REGIONAL AGENCIES: TWO TYPES, TWO DIFFERENT FUNCTIONS

As the problems facing California become more difficult to solve at the city or county level, regional agencies continue their efforts to improve air and water quality, increase transportation options, and manage other "quality of life" concerns. There are two kinds of regional agencies: multi-issue and single-issue.

The *multi-issue regional agencies*, funded primarily by federal monies, try to coordinate the tasks and plans of all the various local government units in a region. The five largest intergovernmental "councils of government" are the Association of Bay Area Governments (ABAG), including nine counties and 100 cities in the San Francisco area; the Southern California Association of Governments (SCAG), embracing six counties and 180 cities; the Sacramento Area Council of Governments (SACOG), including four counties and part of a fifth; the Association of Monterey Bay Area Governments (AMBAG), representing three counties and 20 cities; and the San Diego Association of Governments (SANDAG), including all 18 cities and the county itself. Historically, these agencies have had no authority to enforce their recommendations, so their "advisory" role has often been ignored by the cities and counties they represent.

Perhaps because of the minimal powers of the multi-issue regional agencies, *single-issue regional agencies*, or large special districts, have developed. Air Quality Management Districts with substantial regulatory powers have been established for Southern California, the San Joaquin Valley, and the San Francisco Bay Area, while water supplies for the southern half of the state are handled through the Metropolitan Water District. Transportation in the Bay Area is handled through the Bay Area Rapid Transit District (BART), while the Los Angeles area is served by METRO (MTA).

Although issues such as air pollution or traffic congestion do not stop and start at city or county boundaries, California's regional agencies have not been very successful in developing broad solutions. A major obstacle to regional problem solving is that regional coordination reduces the autonomy of cities and counties, and Californians value their traditions of "local control." Unfortunately, this deep desire for local power and control may not be appropriate to the huge population of today or to the increasing traffic, pollution, and other "quality of life" issues that aggravate Californians.

QUESTIONS TO CONSIDER

Using Your Text and Your Own Experiences

1. Describe the responsibilities of counties and their funding base. What are the financial challenges facing California counties?

2. Define *special districts* and give several examples. Does California need to revise its approach to providing services through special districts? Explain your answer.

3. Why do regional agencies exist? What responses do they encounter as they attempt to create regional solutions to problems?

ENDNOTES

1. California Constitution Revision Commission, *Final Report and Recommendations to the Governor and Legislature,* Sacramento, 1996, p. 72.
2. "Government in California: Buckling under the Strain," *The Economist,* 13 February 1993, p. 21.
3. California Constitution Revision Commission, p. 74.

■ ■ ■ ■ ■

CHAPTER FIFTEEN

Challenges for California's Future

"In contemporary California, for democracy to be
meaningful it must consider all people residing in the state
as potential citizens. A modern democracy cannot survive
when there are entire categories of excluded people."
—Stephanie S. Pincetl, professor of environmental studies[1]

California moves forward into the twenty-first century with a growing
population in need of housing, education, transportation, water, and
energy—all necessities that are not easily provided if government is
frozen in old structures and thinking. While some people continue to
enjoy the material success that has often defined the California dream,
others continue to experience the dream as a myth (see Figure 15.1). With
a polarized political system, in which "no new taxes" battles with "serve
the people," the issue of how to move all Californians forward remains
highly partisan and unresolved.

THE CHALLENGES AHEAD: IT'S
THE ECONOMY, AS USUAL

California's location continues to give the state an edge in the global economy. Positioned next to Mexico and with busy harbors ready for ships
from the Far East, California benefits more than most states from the
increasing trade relations between nations. However, the related risk is
that when the economies of other nations decline, the state loses some of
the advantages of being a major import/export source. And when the
nation's economy is suffering from major federal debts and increasing
commitments to foreign military interventions, even the most prosperous

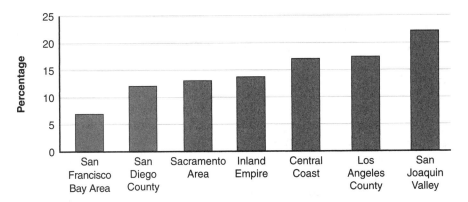

FIGURE 15.1 **Regional Poverty Rates in California, 2000**
Source: American Farmland Trust, *Alternatives for Future Urban Growth in California's Central Valley.*

state cannot always pull itself out of economic distress. Recent federal budget cuts took $1.7 billion from California, creating reductions in health care and education programs.[2]

California is challenged by *globalization,* in which more jobs are *outsourced* while it grows increasingly dependent on foreign imports. Even its world-renowned entertainment industry finds *runaway production* taking jobs to other states and nations. The problem of job loss is compounded by the continuing concern from the business community that the state's poorly funded K–12 educational system does not produce the kind of skilled workers needed.[3]

Along with educating Californians for the high-tech future, other concerns that must be addressed include the continuing gap between rich and poor; the difficulties created by the cultural diversity that also enriches California life; the conflicts involved in managing a complex ecosystem; and the serious question as to whether or not California is "governable."

CAUSES AND CONSEQUENCES: UNDERSTANDING TODAY'S SITUATION

California's economy remains diverse and full of potential. Employment in government at all levels remains a stable option for those who like relative security, while higher incomes can be gained in private-sector employment such as law, real estate, entertainment, tourism, and trade. Of course, in each sector of the economy, there are low-paying jobs as well as high-income opportunities, with the difference often depending on education. In virtually all of the *service industries,* only the highly educated can move into the upper levels, while those whose education is inadequate usually labor for minimum wage or even less. Even though some workers have gained a "living wage" through local political action, and some home health workers, security guards, and janitors have won union representation (often leading to better wages and benefits), the gaps between rich and poor are well documented. This produces a two-tier economy that drastically skews the social and political system. Voter turnout is always high among the affluent and low among those who are less educated and have lower income. While the upper class votes, the *underclass* often feels powerless and neglects to exercise this right.

Perhaps the lack of political action among the poor can be attributed to their daily struggle to survive. Research indicates that the gap between rich and poor has grown not because the rich are getting richer and the poor are remaining the same, but because of "a decline in the income of poor individuals and households."[4] In low-income families, children of working parents rarely have medical insurance, leaving one in six California children without medical coverage.[5] Housing is scarcely affordable even to the middle class, and those with low incomes can rarely join the California Dream as homeowners.[6] Being poor is difficult, especially in a place where the contrasts with affluence are highly visible. These vast gaps are somewhat similar to the class structure in nondemocratic and nonindustrial societies (the Third World). The political leaders rarely talk about the consequences of the continuing income disparity often because they fear offending those who finance their campaigns.

One contributing factor in this enormous *class gap* is the *regressive* tax system, which taxes the poor a greater share of their income than the rich, in part through subsidizing business and long-time property owners through Proposition 13, and then replacing those tax revenues with utility taxes, sales taxes, college fee increases, and other forms of taxation the poor cannot avoid.

As the industrial economy shifts into a more technologically based system, human adjustments to these changes continue to involve economic and social stress. While new technology brings new opportunities, it also slams the door on many workers. In the growing service sector, technological developments allow fewer people to provide the same services. Entire occupations are near obsolescence, including bank tellers, grocery checkers, and others whose work can be done by computers. While some services must remain in California to serve their customers, others move portions of their business out of state for the same reasons that manufacturers leave. With increasing avenues of communication, including e-mail, the Internet, and fax machines, many businesses can operate in states or even nations where wages are lower and corporate taxes less burdensome while still serving clients inside California. The service sector of the economy, though growing, often provides low-wage jobs such as restaurant servers, hotel maids, and janitors, none of whom earn wages comparable to the skilled blue-collar workers in steel, tires, and automobile assembly which used to be readily available in California.

During good times, when the majority of Californians feel prosperous and secure, there is less obvious prejudice and *scapegoating*. However, during times of economic downturn or insecurity, fears of competition for economic opportunities can cause minor prejudices to become full-fledged ethnic rivalries. As more and more Californians are "new neighbors" with different backgrounds and customs, nearly every ethnic group, including the former majority white population, becomes more concerned for its own survival. Demographic data clearly indicate that California's future is multilingual, multicultural, and multiracial. However, because of a variety of historical and social factors, those who currently vote are mostly white, older, and well-to-do. How the gaps between the "old" California and the "new" California will be closed is not yet known. The challenge is to *acculturate* and assimilate new arrivals without destroying their unique cultural identities and without sacrificing the gains of the American-born population. Part of the solution to this challenge is to provide resources for an outstanding educational system that can help people overcome language barriers, cultural stereotypes, and *ethnocentrism*, as well as teach the technological skills and critical thinking essential for success in today's competitive world.

Cultural diversity can enrich daily life through the mingling of music, food, art, language, and even love (one-sixth of all children born in California have parents whose ethnic backgrounds are different from each other),[7] or it can be used to divide communities and individuals. During periods when the economy is growing, the need to blame usually is reduced, and calls to block the borders and shut down the safety net are heard less frequently. However, it is in the hard times, when jobs are scarce and government revenues are reduced, that political leaders must show their skill and compassion by emphasizing social unity rather than divisive politics of blame. That ability to show compassion and emphasize social unity may increase as political leaders from diverse backgrounds enter the halls of leadership. One sign is the substantial increase in Latino political strength; perhaps that community will set the example for the growing Asian groups. Clearly, all ethnic groups must work toward the common goals of all Californians, rather than emphasize an ugly, divisive approach to solving problems.

Even as Californians struggle to figure out how to live in the most multicultural state in the nation, other problems must not be forgotten. The state's ecosystem continues to require attention even during periods when environmental problems are not in the headlines. Debates over the proper management of California's magnificent natural resources involve numerous special-interest groups as well as many concerned individuals. The continuing destruction of agricultural land to meet the housing and shopping needs of a growing population (see Figure 15.2), the unresolved

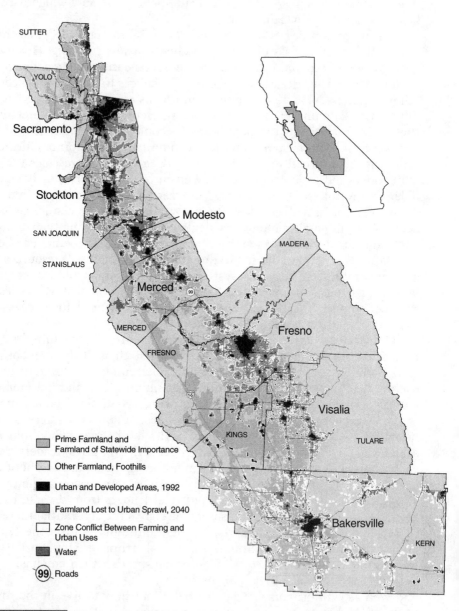

Prime Farmland and
Farmland of Statewide Importance

Other Farmland, Foothills

Urban and Developed Areas, 1992

Farmland Lost to Urban Sprawl, 2040

Zone Conflict Between Farming and
Urban Uses

Water

99 Roads

FIGURE 15.2 **California's Central Valley: Urban Sprawl by 2040**

Source: American Farmland Trust, *Alternatives for Future Urban Growth in California's Central Valley.*

battles over water supplies, the battles over where to dump the inevitable toxic wastes of a chemically dependent economy, and the debates over how to clean California's air and water all contribute to the long list of vital issues that must be faced by elected officials and the public. With little publicity, environmental battles are constantly fought. The skirmishes take place in legislative committees, at community meetings, and at environmentally sensitive sites throughout the state.

In addition to those issues already mentioned, other problems include how to clean up the beaches and bays, how much pesticides can be tolerated on our farms and on our food, how ancient forests can be preserved, where virgin land can be developed, and, in general, how to balance the needs of nature with the needs of the 36 million human beings in the state. The state's environmental progress is also heavily impacted by federal decisions in matters regarding vehicle mileage and emissions standards, appropriate management and use of federal parklands, access to offshore oil drilling, and other environmental matters controlled by federal politics.

Although not every Californian is equally concerned about environmental issues, the long-standing belief that environmentalism is a white, middle-class hobby has been challenged. In fact, it is the underrepresented ethnic groups who often shoulder the burden of environmental damage. Many of the state's toxic waste dumps are located in minority communities, and rates of asthma and other respiratory diseases are worse in inner cities than in suburbs. Latinos lead the state's ethnic groups in their concern about the environment, with air pollution being the number one issue for all Californians.[8] While *environmental racism* is not a common term, it indicates that ethnic minorities often live in the worst ecological circumstances. (Figure 15.3 shows income distributions for California's major population groups.)

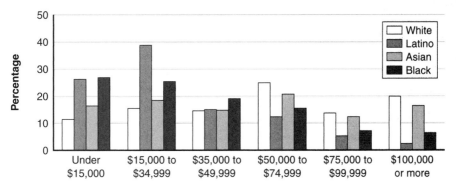

FIGURE 15.3 **Distribution of Family Income in California, 1998**
Source: Public Policy Institute of California.

The growing environmental concerns in communities of color include questions about lead residues in residential housing, water quality in urban areas, and asbestos in public facilities. While everyone tends to support a clean environment, the issue of who pays the cost of cleaning up our society's mess continues to be controversial.

IS CALIFORNIA GOVERNABLE?

Facing such enormous challenges, California needs good political leadership more than ever. Deciding how to respond to national and global economic changes, integrate the increasingly diverse population, provide adequate education and other services to all Californians, regulate business enough to protect people and their environment yet keep corporations from leaving the state, protect irreplaceable natural resources—all of these tasks face a divided state government, which often appears most concerned about its own perks and privileges. Divisions abound—within the parties and between them, between the "oldtimers" and the "newcomers" in government, and among the many special-interest groups that manipulate so much of the decision-making process. To some extent, these conflicts represent inevitable clashes of legitimate, yet contradictory, perspectives. But the average Californian, trying to earn a living, enjoy a family, and find some security for the future, often appears to have faded from the minds of those in power.

Until each of us recognizes the unique opportunities of the state and joins with other concerned citizens to right the existing wrongs, it may well be that the Golden State will never again fully reflect the historic California Dream. That would be a profound disservice to the Californians of today and those of tomorrow. We can only hope that Californians will pull together to avoid this tragic outcome. Californians of all backgrounds must strive to ensure that all ethnic and cultural groups participate and that all elected officials increase their responsiveness to the public (and perhaps reduce their level of service to narrow special-interest groups). No one group can dominate in a state that no longer has a single majority group. It will be the responsibility of the most educated and concerned members of every group to mobilize their friends and associates to join in active, organized efforts to improve life in California.

Unless the general public understands these challenges and the individual's role in them, the future will never be as golden as the state's historic promise. Everyone, to varying degrees, uses the services provided through our state and local governments: airports, highways, beaches, schools, disability checks, community college classes, libraries, drivers licenses, professional licenses, county hospitals—the list is endless. All of us must remember that these services require public money that must be allocated carefully and spent wisely. Those who protest endlessly about paying their share must remember the part of the American ethic which says "United we stand, divided we fall." No Californian can be an island; each and every one must share the benefits and pay the costs of life in California, the cutting edge of the nation.

QUESTIONS TO CONSIDER

Using Your Text and Your Own Experiences

1. What are some of the strengths and weaknesses of today's economy? What can state government do to enhance the economic well-being of the state's people? Should government be involved in promoting economic well-being?
2. What are some strengths and weaknesses of California's political and social circumstances? Who benefits and who loses in the current system? How are you affected by this situation?
3. What can you do to make California a better place to live?

ENDNOTES

1. Stephanie S. Pincetl, *Transforming California: A Political History of Land Use and Development* (Baltimore, MD: Johns Hopkins University Press, 1999), p. 318.
2. Richard Simon and Joel Havemann, "State Takes Hit in Budget," *Los Angeles Times*, 2 February 2006, p. A1.
3. Marla Dickerson, "Problems Seen for High-Tech Economy," *Los Angeles Times*, 17 September 2002, p. C2.
4. Deborah Reed, "Income Inequality in California Outpaces U.S.," Public Affairs Report, Public Policy Institute of California, September 1996, p. 3.
5. Julie Marquis, "'Shocking' Lack Cited in Child Health Insurance," *Los Angeles Times*, 3 March 1997, p. B1.
6. Diane Wedner, "California Home Sales, Prices Post Records in May," *Los Angeles Times*, 27 June 2000, p. C1.
7. Bettina Boxall and Ray F. Herndon, "Far from Urban Gateways, Racial Lines Blur in Suburbs," *Los Angeles Times*, 15 August 2000, p. A1.
8. Nancy Vogel, "Pollution Concerns Latinos More than Most Residents, Poll Finds," *Los Angeles Times*, 22 June 2000, p. A3.

APPENDIX A

Directory of Political Organizations That Anyone Can Join

American Independent Party
(conservative minor party)
1084 W. Marshall Blvd.
San Bernardino, CA 92405
www.aipca.org

Anti-Defamation League
(antidiscrimination, antibigotry)
7851 Mission Center Court #320
San Diego, CA 92108
www.adl.org

Asian Pacific American Legal Center
(civil rights issues)
5 Wilshire Blvd.
Los Angeles, CA 90017
www.apanet.org

California Abortion Rights Action
League (pro-choice)
8455 Beverly Blvd. Suite 303
Los Angeles, CA 90048
www.choice.org

California Coalition for Investor
Responsibility (investing public
pension funds responsibly)
1215 K St. Suite 1920
Sacramento, CA 95814

California Public Interest Research
Group (CALPIRG) (consumer and
environmental issues)
3435 Wilshire #308
Los Angeles, CA 90010
www.pirg.org/calpirg

California Rural Legal Assistance
Fund (legal help in rural areas)
2115 Kern St.
Fresno, CA 93721
www.crla.org

California Tomorrow (making
diversity work/ children's issues)
436 14th St.
Oakland, CA 94612
www.californiatomorrow.org

California Voter Foundation
(using the Web to be
informed)
2401 L St.
Sacramento, CA 95816
www.calvoter.org

Children Now—California
(children's health,
education, etc.)
1212 Broadway, 5th floor
Oakland, CA 94612
www.childrennow.org

Coalition Against Police Abuse
(police behavior issues)
2824 S. Western Ave.
Los Angeles, CA 90018

Coalition for Clean Air (air
quality issues)
10780 Santa Monica Blvd.
Los Angeles, CA 90025
www.coalitionforcleanair.org

Coalition for Economic Survival
(tenants' rights)
1296 N. Fairfax Ave.
West Hollywood, CA 90046

Common Cause (quality of
government issues)
926 J St.
Sacramento, CA 95814
www.commoncause.org

Democratic Party of California
(partisan)
911 20th St.
Sacramento, CA 95814
www.ca-dem.org

Gay and Lesbian Alliance Against
Defamation (monitoring
homophobia in media)
8455 Beverly Blvd. #305
Los Angeles, CA 90048
www.glaad.org

Green Party (environmental
justice/nonviolence)
1008 10th St. #482
Sacramento, CA 95814
www.greens.org/california

Handgun Control Inc. (gun control
lobby)
703 Market St. #1511
San Francisco, CA 94103
www.handguncontrol.org

Health Access (affordable health care
for Californians)
942 Market St. #402
San Francisco, CA 94102

Japanese American Citizens League
(civil rights)
1765 Sutter St.
San Francisco, CA 94115
www.jacl.org

JERICHO: A Voice for Justice (social
justice issues)
926 J ST.
Sacramento, CA 95814

Labor/Community Strategy Center
(environmental/social justice)
3780 Wilshire Blvd., Suite 1200
Los Angeles, CA 90010
www.thestrategycenter.org

League of Conservation Voters—
California (environmental)
1212 Broadway, Suite 630
Oakland, CA 94612
www.lcv.org

League of Women Voters of California
(nonpartisan political reform issues)
926 J St. #515
Sacramento, CA 95814
www.smartvoter.org

Libertarian Party of California
(antigovernment minor party)
655 Lewelling Blvd., Suite 362
San Leandro, CA 94579
www.lp.org

Liveable Wage Coalition (reducing
poverty)
660 Sacramento St. #202
San Francisco, CA 94111

Mexican American Legal Defense
and Education Foundation
(civil rights)
660 Market St.
San Francisco, CA 94194
www.maldef.org

National Association for the
Advancement of Colored People
(one of the first civil rights groups)
3910 W. Martin Luther King Jr. Blvd.
Los Angeles, CA 90008
www.naacp.org

National Conference for Community
and Justice (diversity training,
human relations)
3258 Fourth Ave.
San Diego, CA 92103
www.nccj.org

National Organization for Women
(women's issues)
926 J St. #523
Sacramento, CA 95814
www.now.org

Natural Law Party (meditation as
political action)
P.O. Box 50843
Palo Alto, CA 94303
www.natural-law.org/California.html

Planned Parenthood of California
(family planning lobby)
2415 K St.
Sacramento, CA 95816
www.plannedparenthood.org

Planning and Conservation League
(environmental issues)
926 J St.
Sacramento, CA 95814
www.pcl.org

Republican Party of California
(partisan)
1903 W. Magnolia Blvd.
Burbank, CA 91505
www.cagop.org

Sierra Club (environmental issues)
2530 San Pablo Ave.
Berkeley, CA 94702
www.sierraclub.org

Southern California Library for
Social Studies and Research
(social movement
documents/conferences)
6120 S. Vermont Ave.
Los Angeles, CA 90044
www.socallib.org

Southwest Voter Research/William C.
Velasquez Institute (encourage
Latino voting and political action)
2914 N. Main St., 2nd floor
Los Angeles, CA 90031
800–222–5654
www.svrep.org

Traditional Values Group
(conservative Christian lobby)
1127 11th St.
Sacramento, CA 95814
www.traditionalvalues.org

The Utility Reform Network (TURN)
(consumer advocacy)
711 Van Ness, Suite 350
San Francisco, CA 94105
www.turn.org

United Students Against Sweatshops
(globalization issues)
310 8th St.
Oakland, CA 94607
www.sweatshopwatch.org

APPENDIX B

California State Offices

(All area codes 916 unless otherwise noted)

Governor

Arnold Schwarzenegger (R)
Elected: 2003
Term Limit: 2010
http://www.governor.ca.gov/state/
govsite/gov_homepage.jsp
1st Floor State Capitol
Sacramento 95814
445–2841
Fax: 445–4633

300 S Spring St #16701
Los Angeles 90013
(213) 897–0322
Fax: (213) 897–0319

455 Golden Gate Av #14000
San Francisco 94102
(415) 703–2218
Fax: (415) 703–2803

1350 Front St #6054
San Diego 92101
(619)525–4641
Fax: (619) 525–4640

2550 Mariposa Mall #3013
Fresno 93721
(559) 445–5295
Fax: (559) 445–5328

3737 Main St #201
Riverside 92501
(909) 680–6860
Fax: (909) 680–6863

444 N Capitol St NW
Washington 20001
(202) 624–5270
Fax: (202) 624–5280

Cabinet

Susan Kennedy, Chief of Staff
445–2841

Michael Genest, Dir of Department of Finance
445–3878

A.G. Kawamura, Secy of Department of Food and Agriculture
654–0433

Thomas Johnson, Secy of Department of Veterans Affairs
653–2158

Sunne Wright McPeak, Secy of Business, Transportation and Housing Agency
323–5400

Alan Bersin, Secy of Office of the Secy of Education
323–0611

Alan C. Lloyd, Secy of California Environmental Protection Agency
323–2514

S. Kimberly Belshe, Secy of Health and Human Services Agency
654–3454

Victoria Bradshaw, Secy of Labor and Workforce Development Agency
327–9064

Mike Chrisman, Secy for Resources of Resources Agency
653–5656

Rosario Marin, Secy of State and Consumer Services Agency
653–2636

Rodrick Q. Hickman, Secy of Youth and Adult Correctional Agency
323–6001

Special Offices

Department of Finance
Dir: Michael Genest
http://www.dot.ca.gov
Capitol Building #1145
Sacramento 95814
445–3878
Fax: 324–7311

Department of Food and Agriculture
Secy: A.G. Kawamura
http://www.cdfa.ca.gov
1220 N St #400
Sacramento 95814
654–0433
Fax: 654–0403

Department of Veterans Affairs
Secy: Thomas Johnson
http://www.cdva.ca.gov
1227 0 St
Sacramento 95814
653–2158
Fax: 653–2456

Office of Administrative Law
Dir: William Gausewitz
http://www.oal.ca.gov
300 Capitol Mall #1250
Sacramento 95814
323–6225
Fax: 323–6826

Governor's Office of Emergency Services
Dir: Henry Renteria
http://www.oes.ca.gov
3650 Schriever Ave
Mather 95655
845–8510
Fax: 845–8511

California Film Commission
Exec Dir: Amy Lemisch
http://film.ca.gov
7080 Hollywood Blvd #900
Hollywood 90028
(323) 860–2960
Fax: (323) 860–2972

Military Department, State of California
Adj Gen: William H. Wade II, Major General
http://www.calguard.ca.gov
9800 Goethe Rd Box 269101
Sacramento 95826–9101
854–3000
Fax: 854–3341

Department of Personnel Administration
Dir: Michael T. Navarro
http://www.dpa.ca.gov
1515 S St No Bldg #400
Sacramento 95814–7243
322–5193
Fax: 322–8376

Office of Planning and Research
Act Dir: Sean T. Walsh
http://www.opr.ca.gov
Box 3044
Sacramento 95812–3044
322–2318
Fax: 324–9936

State Public Defender
State Pub Def: Michael Hersek
http://www.ospd.ca.gov
221 Main St 10th Flr
San Francisco 94105
(415) 904–5600
Fax: (415) 904–5635

Lieutenant Governor

John Garamendi (D)
Elected: 2006
Term Limit: 2014
http://www.ltg.ca.gov
Capitol Building #1114
Sacramento 95814
445–8994
Fax: 323–4998

Attorney General
Jerry Brown (D)
Elected: 2006
Term Limit: 2014
http://www.ag.ca.gov
1300 1 St
Sacramento 95814
445–9555

Secretary of State
Debra Bowen (D)
Elected: 2006
Term Limit: 2014
http://www.ss.ca.gov
1500 11th St
Sacramento 95814–5701
653–7244
Fax: 653–4620

Treasurer
Bill Lockyer (D)
Elected 2006
Term Limit: 2014
http://www.treasurer.ca.gov
915 Capitol Mall #110
Sacramento 95814
653–2995
Fax: 653–3125

Controller
John Chiang (D)
Elected: 2006
Term Limit: 2014
http://www.sco.ca.gov
300 Capitol Mall 18th Flr
Sacramento 95814
445–3028
Fax: 322–4404

State Superintendent of Public Instruction
Jack T. O'Connell
Elected: 2002
Term Limit: 2010
http://www.cde.ca.gov
1430 N St #5602
Sacramento 95814–5901

319–0800
Fax: 319–0100

Insurance Commissioner
Steve Poizner (R)
Elected: 2006
Term Limit: 2014
http://www.insurance.ca.gov
300 Capitol Mall #1700
Sacramento 95814
492–3500
Fax: 445–5280

STATE DEPARTMENTS
(All area codes 916 unless otherwise noted)

Business, Transportation and Housing Agency
Agency Secy: Sunne Wright McPeak
http://www.bth.ca.gov
980 9th St #2450
Sacramento 95814–3520
323–5400
Fax: 323–5440

Department of Alcoholic Beverage Control
Dir: Jerry R. Jolly
http://www.abc.ca.gov
3927 Lennane Dr #100
Sacramento 95834
419–2500
Fax: 419–2599

Department of Corporations
Commissioner: William P. Wood
http://www.corp.ca.gov
1515 K St #200
Sacramento 95814–4052
445–7205
Fax: 445–7975

Department of Financial Institutions
Commissioner: Brian Yuen
http://www.dfi.ca.gov
111 Pine St #1100

San Francisco 94111–5613
(415) 263–8500
Fax: (415) 989–5310

California Highway Patrol
Commissioner: Michael Brown
http://www.chp.ca.gov
2555 1st Ave
Sacramento 95818
657–7152
Fax: 657–7324

**Department of Housing and
Community Development**
Dir: Judy Nevis
http://www.hcd.ca.gov
1800 Third St
Sacramento 95814
445–4775
Fax: 324–5107

California Housing Finance Agency
Exec Dir: Theresa A. Parker
http://www.calhfa.ca.gov
1415 L St 5th Flr
Sacramento 95814
322–3991
Fax: 324–8640

**Department of Managed
Health Care**
Dir: Lucinda Ehnes
http://www.hmohelp.ca.gov
980 9th St #500
Sacramento 95814–2725
(888) 466–2219
Fax: 322–9430

Department of Motor Vehicles
Dir: Vacant
Asst Dir, Legislation: Bill Cather
http://www.dmv.ca.gov
2415 1st Ave
Sacramento 95818
657–6518
Fax: 457–7582

Department of Real Estate
Commissioner: Jeffrey M. Davi
http://www.dre.ca.gov
2201 Broadway
Sacramento 95818
227–0782
Fax: 227–0777

Office of Real Estate Appraisers
Act Dir: Anthony F. Majewski
http://www.orea.ca.gov
1102 Q St #4100
Sacramento 95814
440–7878
Fax: 440–7406

**Department of Technology
Services**
Dir: P.K. Agarwal
http://www.dts.ca.gov
Box 1810
Rancho Cordova 95741–1810
464–3400
Fax: 464–4025

Office of Traffic Safety
Act Dir: Christopher J. Murphy
http://www.ots.ca.gov
7000 Franklin Blvd #440
Sacramento 95823–1899
262–0990
Fax: 262–2960

**Department of
Transportation/Caltrans**
Dir: Will Kempton
http://www.dot.ca.gov
1120 N St #1100
Sacramento 95814
654–5266
Fax: 654–6608

California Environmental Protection Agency
Agency Secy: Alan C. Lloyd
http://www.calepa.ca.gov
1001 1St
Sacramento 95814
323–2514
Fax: 324–0908

Air Resources Board
Chair: Dr. Robert Sawyer
http://www.arb.ca.gov/
homepage.htm
1001 1St
Sacramento 95814
322–2990
Fax: 445–5025

Office of Environmental Health Hazard Assessment
Dir: Joan E. Denton, Ph.D.
http://www.oehha.ca.gov
1001 1 St Box 4010
Sacramento 95812–4010
324–7572
Fax: 327–1097

Integrated Waste Management Board
Chair: Vacant
Exec Dir: Mark Leary
http://www.ciwmb.ca.gov
1001 1 St
Sacramento 95814
341–6000
Fax: 341–6054

Department of Pesticide Regulation
Dir: Mary-Ann Warmerdam
http://www.cdpr.ca.gov
1001 1 St
Sacramento 95814
445–4300
Fax: 324–1452

Department of Toxic Substances Control
Dir: Maureen Gorsen
http://www.dtsc.ca.gov
1001 1 St
Sacramento 95814–2828
322–0504
Fax: 327–0978

Water Resources Control Board
Chair: Tam Doduc
Exec Dir: Celeste Cantu
http://www.waterboards.ca.gov
1001 1 St
Sacramento 95814
341–5250
Fax: 341–5621

Health and Human Services Agency
Agency Secy: S. Kimberly Belshe
http://www.chhs.ca.gov
1600 9th St #460
Sacramento 95814–6404
654–3454
Fax: 654–3343

Department of Aging
Dir: Lora Connolly
http://www.aging.ca.gov
1300 National Dr #200
Sacramento 95834
928–7500
Fax: 928–2267

Department of Alcohol and Drug Programs
Dir: Kathryn P. Jett
http://www.adp.ca.gov
1700 K St 5th Flr
Sacramento 95814–4037
445–1943
Fax: 323–5873

Department of Child Support Services
Dir: Greta Wallace
http://www.childsup.cahwnet.gov
Box 419064
Rancho Cordova 95741–9064
(866) 249–0773
Fax: 454–5211

Department of Community Services and Development
Dir: Wendy Wohi
http://www.csd.ca.gov
700 N 10th St #258
Sacramento 95814
341–4200
Fax: 327–3153

Department of Developmental Services
Dir: Cliff Allenby
http://www.dds.cahwnet.gov
1600 9th St #240 MS:2–13
Sacramento 95814
654–1897
Fax: 654–2167

Emergency Medical Services Authority
Interim Dir: Richard E. Watson
http://www.emsa.ca.gov
1930 9th St
Sacramento 95814
322–4336
Fax: 324–2875

Department of Health Services
Dir: Sandra Shewry
http://www.dhs.cahwnet.gov

1501 Capitol Ave #6001
Sacramento 95814
440–7400
Fax: 440–7404

Health and Human Services Data Center
Chf Dpty Dir: Bob Austin
http://www.hwdc.cahwnet.gov
Box 168025
Sacramento 95816
739–7500
Fax: 739–7933

Managed Risk Medical Insurance Board
Chair: Cliff Allenby
Exec Dir: Lesley Cummings
http://www.mrmib.ca.gov
1000 G St #450
Sacramento 95814
324–4695
Fax: 324–4878

Department of Mental Health
Dir: Stephen W. Mayberg, Ph.D.
http://www.dmh.ca.gov
1600 9th St #151
Sacramento 95814
654–2309
Fax: 654–3198

Department of Rehabilltation
Dir: Catherine Campisi, Ph.D.
http://www.rehab.cahwnet.gov
2000 Evergreen St
Sacramento 95815
263–8987
Fax: 263–7474

Department of Social Services
Dir: Cliff Allenby
http://www.dss.cahwnet.gov
744 P St #1740
Sacramento 95814
445–6995
Fax: 445–7333

Office of Statewide Health Planning and Development
Dir: David M. Carlisle. M.D, Ph.D.
http://www.oshpd.state.ca.us
1600 9th St #433

Sacramento 95814
654–1606
Fax: 653–1448

Labor and Workforce Development Agency

Agency Secy: Victoria Bradshaw
http://www.labor.ca.gov
801 K St #2101
Sacramento 95814
327–9064
Fax: 327–9158

Agricultural Labor Relations Board
Chair: Genevieve A. Shiroma
Gen Cnsl: Ed Blanco
http://www.alrb.ca.gov
915 Capitol Mall 3rd Flr
Sacramento 95814
653–3741
Fax: 653–8750

Employment Development Department
Dir: Patrick Henning
http://www.edd.cahwnet.gov
800 Capitol Mall #5000
Sacramento 95814
654–8210
Fax: 657–5294

Department of Industrial Relations
Dir: Vacant
Chf Dpty Dir: John Rea
http://www.dir.ca.gov
455 Golden Gate Ave
San Francisco 94102
(415) 703–5070
Fax: (415) 703–5058

California Workforce Investment Board (CWIB)
Chair: Larry Gotlieb
Exec Dir: Brian McMahon
http://www.calwia.org
777 12th St #200
Sacramento 95814
324–3425
Fax: 324–3068

Resources Agency

Agency Secy: Mike Chrisman
http://resources.ca.gov
1416 9th St #1311
Sacramento 95814
653–5656
Fax: 653–8102

Department of Boating and Waterways

Dir: Raynor Tsuneyoshi
http://www.dbw.ca.gov
2000 Evergreen St #100
Sacramento 95815–3888
263–4326
Fax: 263–0648

California Coastal Commission

Chair: Meg Caldwell
Exec Dir: Peter Douglas
http://www.coastal.ca.gov
45 Fremont St #2000
San Francisco 94105
(415) 904–5200
Fax: (415) 904–5400

State Coastal Conservancy

Exec Off: Samuel Schuchat
http://www.coastalconservancy.ca.gov
1330 Broadway #1100
Oakland 94612–2530
(510) 286–1015
Fax: (510) 286–0470

Colorado River Board of California

Chair: Lloyd Allen
Exec Dir: Gerald R. Zimmerman
http://crb.ca.gov
770 Fairmont Ave #100
Glendale 91203–1035
(818) 500–1625
Fax: (818) 543–4685

California Conservation Corps

Dir: William Semmes
PIO: Susanne Levitsky
http://www.ccc.ca.gov
1719 24th St
Sacramento 95816
341–3100
Fax: 323–4969

Department of Conservation

Dir: Bridgett Luther
http://www.consrv.ca.gov/index
801 K St 24th Flr
Sacramento 95814
322–1080
Fax: 445–0732

Energy Commission

Chair: Joe Desmond
Exec Dir: B.B. Blevins
http://www.energy.ca.gov
1516 9th St
Sacramento 95814–5512
654–4287

Department of Fish and Game

Dir: Loris "Ryan" Brodorick
http://www.dfg.ca.gov
1416 9th St 12th Flr
Sacramento 95814
653–7667
Fax: 653–7387

Forestry and Fire Protection, State Board of

Chair: Stan L. Dixon
Exec Off: George Gentry
http://www.bof.fire.ca.gov
1416 9th St #1506–14
Sacramento 95814
653–8007
Fax: 653–0989

Department of Forestry and Fire Protection

Dir: Dale Geldert
http://www.fire.ca.gov
Box 944246
Sacramento 94244–2460
653–5121
Fax: 653–4171

Mining and Geology Board

Chair: Allen M. Jones
Exec Off: Vacant
http://www.consrv.ca.gov/smgb
801 K St #2015
Sacramento 95814
322–1082
Fax: 445–0738

Department of Parks and Recreation
Dir: Ruth Coleman
http://www.parks.ca.gov
1416 9th St #1405
Sacramento 95814
653–8380
Fax: 657–3903

San Francisco Bay Conservation and Development Commission
Chair: Sean Randolph, PhD
Exec Dir: Will Travis
http://www.bcdc.ca.gov
50 California St #2600
San Francisco 94111
(415) 352–3600
Fax: (415) 352–3606

Santa Monica Mountains Conservancy
Exec Dir: Joseph T. Edmiston
http://smmc.ca.gov
5750 Ramirez Canyon Rd
Malibu 90265
(310) 589–3200
Fax: (310) 589–3207

California Tahoe Conservancy
Exec Off: Patrick Wright
http://www.tahoecons.ca.gov
1061 3rd St
South Lake Tahoe 95150
(530) 542–5580
Fax: (530) 542–5591

Department of Water Resources
Dir: Lester Snow
http://www.water.ca.gov
1416 9th St #1115–1
Sacramento 95814
653–5791
Fax: 653–5028

Wildlife Conservation Board (Department of Fish and Game)
Chair: Vacant
Exec Dir: Al Wright
http://www.wcb.ca.gov
1807 13th St #103
Sacramento 95814
445–8448
Fax: 323–0280

Office of the Secretary of Education
Agency Secy: Alan Bersin
http://www.ose.ca.gov
1121 L St #600
Sacramento 95814
323–0611
Fax: 323–3753

State and Consumer Services Agency
Agency Secy: Rosario Marin
http://www.scsa.ca.gov
915 Capitol Mall #200
Sacramento 95814
653–2636
Fax: 653–3815

California African American Museum
Exec Dir: Charmaine Jefferson
http://www.caam.ca.gov
600 State Dr Exposition Park
Los Angeles 90037
(213) 744–7432
Fax: (213) 744–2050

Building Standards Commission, California
Exec Dir: Stan Nishimura
http://www.bsc.ca.gov
2525 Natomas Park Dr #130
Sacramento 95833–2936
263–0916
Fax: 263–0959

Department of Consumer Affairs
Dir: Charlene Zettel
http://www.dca.ca.gov
1625 North Market Blvd #S308
Sacramento 95814–6200
574–8200
Fax: 574–8613

Department of Fair Employment and Housing
Dir: Suzanne Ambrose
http://www.dfeh.ca.gov
2218 Kausen Dr #100
Elk Grove 95758
478–7251
Fax: 478–7329

**Fair Employment and Housing
Commission**
Chair: George Woolverton
Act Exec & Legal Aff Secy:
Ann M. Noel
455 Golden Gate #10600
San Francisco 94102–3660
(415) 557–2325
Fax: (415) 557–0855

State Fire Marshal
Fire Marshal: Ruben Grijalva
http://ostm.fire.ca.gov
Box 944246
Sacramento 94244–2460
445–8200
Fax: 445–8509

California Franchise Tax Board
Chair: Steve Westly
Exec Off: Selvi Stanislaus
http://www.ftb.ca.gov
Box 115
Rancho Cordova 95741–0115
845–4543
Fax: 845–3191

Department of General Services
Dir: Ron Joseph
http://www.dgs.ca.gov
707 3rd St
West Sacramento 95605
376–5000
Fax: 376–5018

Office of the Insurance Advisor
Dir: Kathleen Webb
915 Capitol Mall 2nd Flr
Sacramento 95814
657–5022
Fax: 653–3815

California Science Center
Pres: Jeffrey N. Rudolph
http://www.californiasciencecenter.org
700 State Dr
Los Angeles 90037
(323) 724–3623
Fax: (213) 744–2650

State Personnel Board
Pres: William Elkins
Exec Off: Floyd D. Shimomura
http://www.spb.ca.gov

801 Capitol Mall
Sacramento 95814
653–1028
Fax: 653–8147

**Professional Engineers and Land
Surveyors, Board of**
Pres: Cindy Tuttle
Exec Off: Cindi Christenson, P.E.
http://www.dca.ca.gov/pels
2535 Capitol Oaks Dr #300
Sacramento 95833–2944
263–2222
Fax: 263–2246

Psychology, Board of
Pres: Jacqueline B. Horn, PhD
Interim Exec Off: Jeffrey Thomas
http://www.psychboard.ca.gov
1422 Howe Ave #22
Sacramento 95825–3200
263–2699
Fax: 263–2697

State Teachers Retirement System
CEO: Jack Ehnes
http://www.calstrs.ca.gov
7667 Folsom Blvd 3rd Flr
Sacramento 95826
229–3700
Fax: 229–3704

**California Public Employees
Retirement System
(CalPERS)**
Pres: Rob Feckner
CEO: Fred Buenrostro
http://www.calpers.ca.gov
400 P St
Sacramento 95814
795–3829
Fax: 795–3410

Youth and Adult Correctional Agency

Agency Secy: Jeanne Woodford
http://www.yaca.ca.gov
1515 K St #520
Sacramento 95815
323–6001
Fax: 442–2637

Corrections, Board of
Chair: Jeanne Woodford
Exec Dir: Karen L. Stoll
http://www.bdcorr.ca.gov
600 Bercut Dr
Sacramento 95814
445–5073
Fax: 327–3317

Department of Corrections and Rehabilitation
Dir: Jeanne Woodford
http://www.cdcr.ca.gov
1515 S St
Sacramento 95814
445–7682
Fax: 322–2877

Prison Industry Board
Chair: J.S. Woodford
Exec Secy: Vicki Britt
560 E Natoma St
Folsom 95630–2200
358–2677
Fax: 358–1732

Parole Hearings, Board of
Chair: Susan L. Fisher
Exec Off: Dennis M. Kenneally
http://www.cdcr.ca.gov/
   divisions boards/boph/
   index.html
1515 K St #600
Sacramento 95814
445–4072
Fax: 445–5242

Division of Juvenile Justice
Chf Dpty Secy: Bernard Warner
http://www.cya.ca.gov
1515 S St #502 South
Sacramento 95814
323–6001
Fax: 442–2637

Youth Authority Board
Chair: Walter Allen
http://www.yopb.ca.gov
3336 Bradshaw Rd #255
Sacramento 95827–2615
255–4495
Fax: 255–4410

STATE SENATE

President
Lt. Governor John Garamendi (D)

President pro Tempore
Don Perata (D)

Majority Floor Leader
Gloria Romero (D)

Minority Floor Leader
Dick Ackerman (R)

Majority Whip
~~Richard Alarcon~~ (D)

Minority Whip
Dennis Hollingsworth (R)

Democratic Caucus Chair
Tom Torlakson

Republican Caucus Chair
George Runner

Sam Aanestad (R–4)
Term Limit: 2010
Nevada City

Dick Ackerman (R–33)
Term Limit: 2008
Tustin

Alex Padilla (D–20)
Term Limit: 2014
Van Nuys

Elaine Alquist (D–13)
Term Limit: 2012
San Jose

Roy Ashburn (R–18)
Term Limit: 2010
Bakersfield

Jim Battin (R–37)
Term Limit: 2008
Palm Desert

Jenny Oropeza (D–28)
Term Limit: 2014
Redondo Beach

Gilbert Cedillo (D–22)
Term Limit: 2010
Los Angeles

Patricia Wiggins (D–2)
Term Limit: 2014
Santa Rosa

Dave Cox (R–1)
Term Limit: 2012
Roseville

Jeff Denham (R–12)
Term Limit: 2010
Modesto

Denise Moreno Ducheny (D–40)
Term Limit: 2010
Chula Vista

Lyn Daucher (R–34)
Term Limit: 2014
Garden Grove

Bob Dutton (R–31)
Term Limit: 2012
Rancho Cucamonga

Ron Calderon (D–30)
Term Limit: 2014
Norwalk

Ellen Corbett (D–10)
Term Limit: 2014
Fremont

Dean Florez (D–16)
Term Limit: 2010
Bakersfield

Dennis Hollingsworth (R–36)
Term Limit: 2010
Temecula

Christine Kehoe (D–39)
Term Limit: 2012
San Diego

Sheila Kuehl (D–23)
Term Limit: 2008
Los Angeles

Alan S. Lowenthal (D–27)
Term Limit: 2012
Long Beach

Michael J. Machado (D–5)
Term Limit: 2008
Stockton

Abel Maldonado (R–15)
Term Limit: 2012
San Luis Obispo

Bob Margett (R–29)
Term Limit: 2008
Glendora

Tom McClintock (R–19)
Term Limit: 2008
Thousand Oaks

Carole Migden (D–3)
Term Limit: 2012
San Francisco

Mark Wyland (R–38)
Term Limit: 2014
San Juan Capistrano

Mark Ridley-Thomas (D–26)
Term Limit: 2014
Culver City

Darrell Steinberg (D–6)
Term Limit: 2014
Sacramento

Don Perata (D–9)
Term Limit: 2014
Oakland

Dave Cogdill (R–14)
Term Limit: 2014
Fresno

Gloria Romero (D–24)
Term Limit: 2010
Los Angeles

George C. Runner (R–17)
Term Limit: 2012
Lancaster

Jack Scott (D–21)
Term Limit: 2008
Pasadena

S. Joseph Simitian (D–11)
Term Limit: 2012
Palo Alto

Gloria Negrete McLeod (D–32)
Term Limit: 2014
Ontario

Leland Yee (D–8)
Term Limit: 2014
San Mateo

Tom Tortakson (D–7)
Term Limit: 2008
Concord

Edward Vincent (D–25)
Term Limit: 2008
Inglewood

STATE ASSEMBLY

Speaker
Fabian Nunez (D)

Speaker pro Tem
Leland Yee (D)

Majority Floor Leader
Dario Frommer (D)

Minority Floor Leader
Kevin McCarthy (R)

Majority Whip
Karen Bass (D)

Minority Whip
John Benoit (R)

Democratic Caucus Chair
Mark Ridley-Thomas

Republican Caucus Chair
Russ Bogh

Greg Aghazarian (R–26)
Term Limit: 2008
Stockton

Juan Arambula (D–31)
Term Limit: 2010
Fresno

Joe Baca Jr. (D–62)
Term Limit: 2010
San Bernardino

Karen Bass (D–47)
Term Limit: 2010
Los Angeles

John J. Benoit (R–64)
Term Limit: 2008
Riverside

Patty Berg (D–1)
Term Limit: 2008
Santa Rosa

Rudy Bermudez (D–56)
Term Limit: 2008
Norwalk

Sam Blakeslee (R–33)
Term Limit: 2010
San Luis Obispo

Paul Cook (R–65)
Term Limit: 2012
Yucaipa

Ronald Calderon (D–58)
Term Limit: 2008
Montebello

Mark DeSaulnier (D–11)
Term Limit: 2012
Martinez

Sandre Swanson (D–16)
Term Limit: 2012
Oakland

Ed Hernandez (D–57)
Term Limit: 2012
City of Industry

Mike Eng (D–49)
Term Limit: 2012
Monterey Park

Tom Berryhill (R–25)
Term Limit: 2012
Modesto

Jim Beall (D–24)
Term Limit: 2012
San Jose

Joe Coto (D–23)
Term Limit: 2010
San Jose

Mike Duvall (R–72)
Term Limit: 2012
Brea

Hector De La Torre (D–50)
Term Limit: 2010
South Gate

Chuck DeVore (R–70)
Term Limit: 2010
Irvine

Mervyn Dymally (D–52)
Term Limit: 2008
Compton

Bill Emmerson (R–63)
Term Limit: 2010
Rancho Cucamonga

Noreen Evans (D–7)
Term Limit: 2010
Santa Rosa

Paul Krekorian (D–43)
Term Limit: 2012
Glendale

Bonnie Garcia (R–80)
Term Limit: 2008
El Centro

Kevin De Leon (D–45)
Term Limit: 2012
Los Angeles

Loni Hancock (D–14)
Term Limit: 2008
El Cerrito

Jim Silva (R–67)
Term Limit: 2012
Huntington Beach

Kevin Jeffries (R–66)
Term Limit: 2012
Temecula

Curren Price (D–51)
Term Limit: 2012
Inglewood

Shirley Horton (R–78)
Term Limit: 2008
Lemon Grove

Guy Houston (R–15)
Term Limit: 2008
Livermore

Robert "Bob" Huff (R–60)
Term Limit: 2010
Diamond Bar

Dave Jones (D–9)
Term Limit: 2010
Sacramento

Betty Karnette (D–54)
Term Limit: 2008
Long Beach

Rick Keene (R–3)
Term Limit: 2008
Chico

Johan Klehs (D–18)
Term Limit: 2010
Hayward

Mike Feuer (D–42)
Term Limit: 2012
West Hollywood

Doug La Malfa (R–2)
Term Limit: 2008
Redding

Joel Anderson (R–77)
Term Limit: 2012
La Mesa

John Laird (D–27)
Term Limit: 2008
Santa Cruz

Mark Leno (D–13)
Term Limit: 2008
San Francisco

Ted Gaines (R–4)
Term Limit: 2012
Roseville

Lloyd Levine (D–40)
Term Limit: 2008
Van Nuys

Sally Lieber (D–22)
Term Limit: 2008
Mountain View

Ted W. Lieu (D–53)
Term Limit: 2012
El Segundo

Anthony Portantino (D–44)
Term Limit: 2012
Pasadena

Cathleen Galgiani (D–17)
Term Limit: 2012
Stockton

Bill Maze (R–34)
Term Limit: 2008
Visalia

Kevin McCarthy (R–32)
Term Limit: 2008
Bakersfield

Richard Alarcon (D–39)
Term Limit: 2012
San Femando

Anthony Adams (R–59)
Term Limit: 2012
Monrovia

Gene Mullin (D–19)
Term Limit: 2008
San Mateo

Alan Nakanishi (R–10)
Term Limit: 2008
Lodi

Jared Huffman (D–6)
Term Limit: 2012
San Rafael

Pedro Nava (D–35)
Term Limit: 2010
Santa Barbara

Nell Soto (D–61)
Term Limit: 2012
Montclair

Roger Niello (R–5)
Term Limit: 2010
Sacramento

Fabian Nunez (D–46)
Term Limit: 2008
Los Angeles

Laura Richardson (D–55)
Term Limit: 2012
Carson

Nicole Parra (D–30)
Term Limit: 2008
Bakersfield

Julia Brownley (D–41)
Term Limit: 2012
Woodland Hills

George Plescia (R–75)
Term Limit: 2008
San Diego

Cameron Smyth (R–38)
Term Limit: 2012
Granada Hills

Mike Davis (D–48)
Term Limit: 2012
Los Angeles

Sharon Runner (R–36)
Term Limit: 2008
Lancaster

Ira Ruskin (D–21)
Term Limit: 2010
Los Altos

Lori Saldana (D–76)
Term Limit: 2010
San Diego

Anna Marie Caballero (D–28)
Term Limit: 2012
Salinas

Todd Spitzer (R–71)
Term Limit: 2008
Orange

Audra Strickland (R–37)
Term Limit: 2010
Westlake Village

Alberto Torrico (D–20)
Term Limit: 2010
Fremont

Van Tran (R–68)
Term Limit: 2010
Costa Mesa

José Solorio (D–69)
Term Limit: 2012
Anaheim

Mary Salas (D–79)
Term Limit: 2012
Chula Vista

Mike Villines (R–29)
Term Limit: 2010
Fresno

Mimi Walters (R–73)
Term Limit: 2010
Laguna Niguel

Lois Wolk (D–8)
Term Limit: 2008
Vacaville

Martin Garrick (R–74)
Term Limit: 2012
Vista

Fiona Ma (D–12)
Term Limit: 2012
San Francisco

APPENDIX C

Useful Web Sites

California State Home Page:
www.ca.gov

California State Senate:
www.senate.ca.gov

California State Assembly:
www.assembly.ca.gov

California Secretary of State:
www.ss.ca.gov

California Geographical Survey:
goegodata.csun.edu/

California Higher Education
Policy Center:
www.policy center.org

Center for California Studies:
www.csus.edu/calst/index.html

California Voter Foundation:
www.calvoter.org

California Government Agency and
Commission List:
www.ganymede.org/agencies.html

California State Association
of Counties:
www.csac.counties.org

University of California system:
www.ca.gov/s/learning/uc.html

California State University system:
www.ca.gov/s/learning/csu.html

Community College Chancellor's
Office:
www.cccco.edu

California Historical Society:
www.calhist.org

California Court system:
www.courtinfo.ca.gov

California Law References:
www.leginfo.ca.gov/calaw.html

Search Bills in the California
Legislature:
www.sen.ca.gov/www/leginfo/
SearchText.html

Southern California Association of
Governments (SCAG):
www.scg.ca.gov

Association of Bay Area
Governments:
www.abag.ca.gov

League of Women Voters of
California:
www.ca.lwv.org

California Voter Foundation
(candidates/issues):
www.calvoter.org

Center for Responsive Politics
(tracking money in campaigns):
www.opensecrets.org

League of California Cities:
www.cacities.org

California Chamber of Commerce:
www.calchamber.com

California Futures Network
(growth/development issues):
www.calfutures.org

Public Policy Institute of California:
www.ppic.org

Institute for Governmental Studies
UC Berkeley:
www.igs.berkeley.edu:8880

U.S. Census Data:
www.census.gov

Cities Counties Schools:
www.ccspartnership.org

Border Region Information:
www.borderecoweb.sdsu.edu

Community College League of
California:
www.ccleague.org

California Department of
Transportation:
www.dot.ca.gov

California Research Bureau:
www.library.ca.gov

Chicano/Latino Net:
www.clnet.ucr.edu

APPENDIX D

How to Get in Touch with your Elected Officials

Since every Californian is represented by multiple elected officials, it can be confusing to find the one you need. Each of us has two U.S. senators, 1 U.S. House of Representatives member, 1 state senator, and 1 Assembly member, as well as eight constitutional officers (including the governor). Then at the local level, you have a county supervisor, a city council representative (unless you live in an unincorporated area), and numerous school board and community college board representatives.

HOW CAN YOU FIND THE PERSON YOU NEED?

1. Analyze the situation. Do you need a local, state, or federal response? If you wish to express your views on legislation, make sure you know whether it is in Washington, D.C., Sacramento, or your city hall. Get the bill number and author's name.

2. If you need a state official, check Appendix B and skim the list to see if your city or community is listed. All state legislators receive mail at: State Capitol, Sacramento, CA 95814. Due to term limits, the list changes frequently. You can use the Web or local phone book to verify your current representatives.

3. Use your local telephone directory to find out who represents you. Almost all now have listings for "Government Officials" for all three levels of government.

4. Use the Web to find your elected officials. Go to the following sites as needed.
   www.assembly.ca.gov
   www.senate.ca.gov
   www.house.gov/writerep/
   thomas.loc.gov/

5. Verify the name and address by phoning the local office of the elected official.

ONCE YOU KNOW THE NAME AND ADDRESS, FOLLOW THESE STEPS

Address your letter to "Honorable Mr. or Ms. xxx" and use the proper address.

Use your own words to briefly describe your problem, concern, or question. If you are writing to express your views about specific legislation, refer to the bill number and author's name. Be brief and constructive in your comments. Explain your reasons for your views on the issue.

Be sure to include your signature, your printed name, and your full address. Most elected officials will respond to your letter—however, this may take several months.

Remember, most elected officials only get feedback from organized interest groups and their members. Your individual letter is often considered as having the impact of hundreds of people's views. Your letter can make a difference!

Glossary

Acculturate   The process by which immigrants learn their new culture's language, customs, and traditions.

Affirmative Action   A policy designed to enhance opportunities for ethnic or other groups who were denied access in the past, such as African-Americans, Latinos.

Amend   To change a document such as a bill.

Appropriations   Funds allocated by elected officials for public programs.

Assimilation   The process by which a new group learns the rules of the more established group and adopts its customs.

At-large   A method of electing members of a city council or other legislative body by voters in the entire governmental unit rather than in individual districts.

Ballot initiative   See Initiative.

Ballot status   Appearing on the ballot, such as a political party.

Baseline budget   A budget based on the previous year's budget rather than a "zero-based" budget that requires all programs to justify their existence.

Blanket primary   A primary in which all candidates from every party are listed together.

Bond measures   Ballot measures that require voter approval so that the state or local governments may borrow money for land purchases and construction investments (prisons, schools, roads, parks, etc.). Bonds may not be used for operating costs.

Bracero   Legal temporary immigrant worker usually brought from Mexico to work in agriculture.

Californios   During the period following Mexico's loss of California to the United States (1848–1890s) residents of California who were of Mexican descent.

Challenger   In politics, a person who runs against an incumbent.

Civil liberties   Protected types of behavior such as freedom of speech or religion, which governments are prohibited from taking away.

Civil rights   Legally imposed obligations, such as the right to equal protection of the laws or reasonable bail, that governments owe to individuals.

Civil service system   A set of procedures for hiring government employees on the basis of merit, usually demonstrated by examination, and protecting them against unjust firing.

Class gap   An increasing gap in resources between the wealthiest and the poorest people.

Conference committee   A temporary committee appointed to resolve differences between the Senate and Assembly versions of a bill.

Conquistadores   Spanish conquerors in the New World (Western Hemisphere).

Conservative   A political philosophy that favors smaller government, lower taxes, fewer public services, and a "laissez-faire" (let them do as they please) approach to business.

Constitutional offices   The executive offices that the state constitution requires must be elected by the voters.

Contract city   City that purchases police and fire services from the county.

Council–manager   A form of city government in which the elected city council, with legislative authority, appoints, and can fire, a city manager to whom the various executive departments are responsible.

County committee   Also known as county central committee; a group of elected party activists within each county.

Decline to state   A voter's registration status when he or she does not wish to affiliate with any political party.

Defendant   In a civil case, the entity being sued; in a criminal case, the accused person.

Demographic shift   Noticeable changes in population data, including numbers of people, size of ethnic groups, and so on.

Direct democracy   The reforms of the Progressive movement, which enable voters to directly make laws, amend the state constitution, recall officials, or repeal laws passed by elected representatives.

District-based   A city, school district, or other governmental unit is divided into geographic districts, each of which has a representative elected by the voters in that district.

Electoral votes   The number of votes a state may cast in electing the president and vice president, computed by adding the number of its U.S. senators (two) to the number of Representatives (53 for California as of 2000).

Electorate   Those who vote.

Environmental racism   When environmental pollution primarily impacts ethnic minority communities.

Ethnocentrism   The belief that one's own ethnic group is superior to other ethnic groups.

Executive clemency   The governor's power to lighten criminal sentences imposed by the courts by pardons, which cancel them, commutations, which reduce them, or reprieves, which postpone them; amnesties are pardons for an entire group.

Ex-officio   A nonvoting member of a governmental body.

Federalism   A political system in which the national and state systems have some powers independent of each other.

Felonies   The most serious crimes, including murder, rape, and arson.

Franchise   In politics, the right to vote.

Gerrymandering   Manipulation of district boundaries to favor the election of a particular group, individual, or candidate of the dominant political party.

Get out the Vote (GOTV)   Campaign strategies including phone calls, rides to the polls, and free donuts.

GLBT   An acronym for gay, lesbian, bisexual, transgendered.

Globalization   The increasing economic interdependence of many nations.

GOP   Grand Old Party, Republican Party.

Grassroots Pertaining to actions, movements or organizations of a political nature that rely chiefly on the mass involvement of ordinary citizens.

Gubernatorial Pertaining to the office of governor.

Homophobia Fear or hatred of homosexuals.

Image making Creating a positive impression about a candidate through the use of public relations methods and mass media.

Immigrant-bashing The blaming of immigrants, whether legal or undocumented, for social problems.

Incumbent Person currently in office.

Indictment Formal accusation of criminal behavior by a grand jury, sometimes used to bring defendants to trial.

Inflation A situation in which prices increase rapidly.

Infractions Minor criminal offenses, such as jaywalking.

Infrastructure The tangible components that allow society to function: bridges, roads, water systems, sewage systems, and so on.

Initiative The process by which citizens can propose a state or local law or amendment to the state constitution by signing a formal petition asking that it be submitted as a ballot proposition for voter approval.

Interest Groups See special interest groups.

Issue-oriented organizations Groups concerned primarily with political issues, such as abortion, civil rights, medical care, and so forth, as opposed to groups interested in electing specific candidates.

Item veto Sometimes called the line-item veto; the authority of the governor to reduce or eliminate money appropriated by the legislature for a specific purpose while signing the remaining provisions of the bill into law.

Liberal A political philosophy that supports active government involvement in creating a more just society and that supports individual freedoms in personal matters.

Lobbying The attempt to influence government policy, usually on behalf of an interest group.

Majority More than 50 percent.

Mandates Requirements; for example, a federal mandate may require states to take a particular action.

Manifest destiny The justification of U.S. territorial expansion based on the mystical assumption that it was the clear fate of the nation to acquire at least all land between the Atlantic and Pacific oceans.

Maquiladoras Factories on the Mexican side of the border designed to use Mexican labor for goods to be imported to the United States.

Mayor–council A form of city government based on a separation of powers between a mayor with executive authority and the council with legislative authority, both elected by the voters.

Mestizo Of mixed race, particularly Spanish European and pre-Columbian Indian heritage.

Minimalist That which is limited to its simplest or most essential elements; politically, the usually conservative belief that government should do very little.

Misdemeanors An intermediate level of crime, less damaging to persons or property than a felony.

Monocultural electorate A term that describes California's largely white electorate, in contrast with a largely nonwhite population at large.

Multi-issue regional agency Agency that coordinates tasks and plans of all the various local government units in a region, typically in an advisory capacity.

Naturalization The process of becoming a U.S. citizen.

Nonpartisan Elections, such as those of judges, school board members, and city and county officials in California, in which the party affiliation of the candidates does not appear on the ballot.

Office-block ballot To discourage straight-ticket party voting, the arrangement of candidates' names according to the office for which they are running rather than their party affiliation.

Ordinance A law passed by a city or county.

Out of the closet Open about one's gay male or lesbian sexual orientation.

Outsourcing The movement of work outside the state or nation, such as customer service phone calls or the production of goods.

Override When the legislative body votes again on a bill vetoed by the executive and overcomes the veto by a two-thirds majority so that the bill becomes law without the executive's approval.

Partisan Reflecting strong loyalty to a party or political faction.

Partisan election An election in which the party affiliation of the candidates appears on the ballot.

Party affiliation An individual's choice of a party when registering to vote; may or may not include any activity in that party.

Patronage The use of appointment powers to reward political supporters.

Plaintiff The person bringing suit in a civil case.

Plea bargain Negotiations in a criminal case designed to get the defendant to plead guilty if the prosecution reduces the seriousness of the charge or reduces the sentence.

Plurality The most votes.

Polarization A sharp division between groups, such as the increasing differences in views between conservative Republicans and liberal Democrats.

Political action committee (PAC) An organization, usually formed by an interest group or corporation, designed to solicit money from individuals to be used for campaign contributions to candidates endorsed by the group.

Polls The location where votes are cast; in opinion research, surveys of public opinion.

President pro tem The leader of the state Senate, elected by the membership.

Private sector Refers to all business and other activities that are not sponsored directly by government; however, much of the American private sector is subsidized through government funds.

Privatization Any effort to cut back government and substitute private-sector activity: For example, firing public janitors and "contracting out" to a private profit-seeking janitorial service.

Progressive movement The growing demand in the early 1900s for direct democracy options such as initiative, recall, and referendum.

Proposition An item on the ballot that requires a "yes" or "no" vote, including initiative, referendum, recall, and bond issue.

Recall A progressive era reform permitting the voters, by petition, to call a special election to remove an official from office before the next regularly scheduled election.

Recession A period during which the economy slows down, including fewer jobs, higher unemployment, lower consumption, and reduced tax revenues.

Redbaiting During the Cold War, the effort to discredit a person by implying that he or she was a communist ("red").

Redistricting Redrawing the boundaries of election districts; required after each census to keep district populations as nearly equal as possible.

Referendum The type of ballot proposition that allows voters to repeal or revoke laws passed by the legislature.

Regressive In reference to taxation, indicates that the poor are taxed more than the rich in proportion to their incomes.

Repatriation Returning immigrants to their country of origin.

Representative democracy System in which citizens elect representatives to make decisions.

Runaway Production When films are produced outside California, leading to job loss in the state's entertainment industry.

Runoff election An election held when no candidate in a nonpartisan primary receives a majority; the two top candidates enter the "runoff" so that the final winner is elected by a majority vote.

Safe districts Election districts in which one party, through gerrymandering, is virtually guaranteed victory at the polls.

Scapegoating The process of blaming a social/ethnic group for society's problems.

Semi-closed primary A primary in which "decline to state" voters may request a particular party's candidate list, while party members get only their party's ballot choices.

Service industry An industry that does not manufacture anything but rather provides services, such as health care, education, or retail sales.

Settlement Money awarded to a plaintiff through negotiations.

Single-issue regional agency A large special district that provides a service or regulates an area, such as air quality or water supplies.

Speaker of the assembly The presiding officer and most powerful member of the Assembly, elected by the membership.

Special district Local units of government which perform a service that no city or county provides, which may encompass an area larger than any one city or county, and which have their own governing body, either appointed or elected.

Special-interest groups Also known as pressure groups or lobbies; organizations that try to influence politicians to achieve their political and economic aims.

Standing committees Permanent committees of the California Senate and Assembly organized around policy subjects, to which every bill is referred and in which most of the work of legislation occurs.

Statute A law that is in the code books and is not part of an actual constitution or charter.

Swing votes Votes that are not predictable and can be swayed to support candidates or issues.

Target audience A select group of voters who receive political mailings with messages aimed at winning their support.

Tax assessment In reference to property taxes, the amount that must be paid; it is based upon the property's assessed value.

Term limits A rule that permits a politician only a limited number of opportunities to run for the same office. Term limits exist at the state level and in some cities in California.

Two-tier society A society in which there is a small affluent upper class, a large class of impoverished people, including the working poor and the underclass, and a small middle class.

Underclass Those long-term impoverished persons who survive through government assistance, charity, or criminal activity. They should not be confused with the "working poor," although income levels may be similar.

Underrepresented Ethnic or other groups that have historically not had political representation in proportion to their population.

Unincorporated area Territory outside the boundaries of incorporated cities whose residents receive nearly all municipal services from county government.

Unitary In contrast to a federal system, one in which the county and other regional or local governments have only the powers the state gives to them.

Upset An election in which the outcome is a surprise to political observers.

Veto The return of a bill by the chief executive to the legislative body that passed it, unsigned, thereby killing it unless the legislature overrides the veto.

Vote-by-Mail (VBM) An option available to all voters to request a VBM ballot, vote and mail it, and avoid going in person to the polling place on election day.

White flight The process by which whites move away from areas as ethnic minorities begin to move in.

Bibliography

Baldassare, Mark, *A California State of Mind: The Conflicted Voter in a Changing World*, University of California Press, 2002.

Beebe, Rose Marie, and Robert Senkewicz, *Chronicles of Early California: Lands of Promise and Despair, 1535–1846*, Heyday Books, 2001.

Bonacich, Edna, and Richard Appelbaum, *Behind the Label: Inequality in the Los Angeles Apparel Industry*, University of California Press, 2000.

Brechin, Gray, *Imperial San Francisco: Urban Power, Earthly Ruin*, University of California Press, 1999.

Collier, Michael, *A Land in Motion: California's San Andreas Fault*, University of California Press, 1999.

Erie, Steven P., *Globalizing L.A.: Trade, Infrastructure and Regional Development*, Stanford University Press, 2004.

Fradkin, Philip, *The Seven States of California: A Natural and Human History*, University of California Press, 1999.

Fulton, William, *The Reluctant Metropolis: The Politics of Urban Growth in Los Angeles*, Solano Press Books, 1997.

Glantz, Stanton A., and Edith Balbach, *Tobacco War: Inside the California Battle*, University of California Press, 2000.

Gordon, Bernard, *Hollywood Exile or How I learned to Love the Blacklist*, University of Texas Press, 2000.

Gordon, Tracy M., et al., *Fiscal Realities: Budget Tradeoffs for California Government*, Public Policy Institute, 2006.

Griggs, Gary, et al., *Living with the Changing California Coast*, University of California Press, 2005.

Gumprecht, Blake, *The Los Angeles River: Its Life, Death and Possible Rebirth*, Johns Hopkins University Press, 1999.

Gutierrez, Ramon A., and Richard Orsi, *Contested Eden: California Before the Gold Rush*, University of California Press, 1998.

Hanak, Ellen, et al., *California 2025: Taking on the Future*, Public Policy Institute, 2005.

Haslam, Gerald, *Workin' Man Blues: Country Music in California*, University of California Press, 1999.

Hayes-Bautista, David, *La nueva California: Latinos in the Golden State*, University of California Press, 2004.

Hill, Mary, *Gold: The California Story*, University of California Press, 1999.

Hise, Greg, and William Deverell, *Eden by Design: The 1930 Olmsted-Bartholomew Plan for the Los Angeles Region*, University of California Press, 2000.

Lubenow, Gerald, *California Votes: The 2002 Governor's Race and the Recall that Made History*, Berkeley Public Policy Press, Institute of Governmental Studies, 2003.

Marschner, Janice, *California's Arab Americans*, Coleman Ranch Press, 2003.

Martinez, Ruben, *Crossing Over: A Mexican Family on the Migrant Trail*, Metropolitan Books, 2001.

McClung, Sue, *Water and the Shaping of California*, Water Education Foundation, 2000.

McClung, William Alexander, *Landscapes of Desire: Anglo Mythologies of Los Angeles*, University of California Press, 2000.

Merchant, Carolyn, *Green Versus Gold: Sources in California's Environmental History*, Island Press, 1998.

Michael, Jay, and Dan Walters, *The Third House: Lobbyists, Money and Power in Sacramento*, University of California Press, 2002.

Mulholland, Catherine, *William Mulholland and the Rise of Los Angeles*, University of California Press, 2000.

Ochoa, Enrique C., and Gilda L. Ochoa, *Latino Los Angeles: Transformations, Communities, and Activism*, University of Arizona Press, 2005.

Pincetl, Stephanie, *Transforming California: A Political History of Land Use and Development*, Johns Hopkins University Press, 1999.

Pitti, Stephen, *The Devil in Silicon Valley: Northern California, Race and Mexican Americans*, Princeton University Press, 2003.

Reed, Deborah, et al., *Educational Progress Across Immigrant Generations in California*, Public Policy Institute, 2005.

Roderick, Kevin, *The San Fernando Valley: America's Suburb*, Los Angeles Times Books, 2001.

Schiesl, Martin, and Mark Dodge, *City of Promise: Race and Historical Change in Los Angeles*, Regina Books, 2006.

Schrag, Peter, *Paradise Lost: California's Experience, America's Future*, University of California Press, 1998.

Schwartz, Stephen, *From West to East: California and the Making of the American Mind*, Free Press, 1998.

Secrest, William, *When the Great Spirit Died: The Destruction of the California Indians, 1850–1860*, Word Dancer Press, 2003.

Tywoniak, Frances Esquibel, and Mario T. Garcia, *Migrant Daughter: Coming of Age as a Mexican American Woman*, University of California Press, 2000.

Yung, Judy, *Unbound Voices: A Documentary History of Chinese Women in San Francisco*, University of California Press, 1999.

Index